Social Capital 2.0

Dr. Rick L. Mask

DEDICATION

This book is dedicated to all those who seek to once again live in a world where human relationships and communication matter.

CONTENTS

Introduction

I'm glad you opened this book. The message contained here, and the power of the message to better the lives of everyone who reads it, has been a passion of mine for a long time. In our society, I view relationships, and communication in general, as often being stifled by automation, digitization, and social media. These tools ostensibly make our lives easier, but their side-effects have left us with a lack luster face-to-face experience, and degradation of some of the most innately human aspects of life.

We feel this impact in our personal lives and our business lives. We have forgotten the importance of direct communication and the long-term benefits of creating social capital with those around us. Instead of calling someone, we text. Instead of checking in with family, we look at their Facebook newsfeed. Instead of connection, we opt for convenience.

Long-term relationships we build throughout our lives help us to grow, not only as individuals, but in our careers and with our personal business goals. Direct contact must flourish if our society and our businesses are to continue to function at the most effective levels possible. The purpose of the forthcoming is to impart that to you.

Part One: The Basics of Social Capital

Chapter 1: Our Terms

The world has an odd way of seeming to contrive the need for books like the one you are currently reading. Throughout recent years, factors in numerous aspects of everyday American life and business, forces operating on a micro and macro scale, have combined in an almost conspiratorial manner to necessitate the creation of a book preaching the value of social capital. We are living in a world where social capital, once something companies looked to as their greatest resource, is deliberately cast aside in favor of unequal advantages elsewhere. Formerly husbanded delicately as the sole asset with the power to overcome pure economic advantage, social capital has devolved into the forgotten toy in a child's Happy meal. If the business world held an election, social capital has dropped from the plucky challenger, fighting for votes against a tired status quo of price points, to the "also-ran candidate", proclaiming ideas to an uncaring electorate.

However, not unlike many (although certainly not all) second-place political candidates, there is a lot to be said for social capital once you start taking it seriously. This book aims to do exactly that. And, while it may be a difficult turn to imagine social capital above the enticing simplicity of price advantages, you will find that transformation easier the more you read.

When examining something as intricate and imperative as social capital, it is crucial to begin with a clear definition of terms. What are we talking about? Without common language, the greater part of the message this book is trying to convey will be unappreciated or misinterpreted. While economists, sociologists, philosophers, and even teachers have approached social capital in numerous fashions for decades (and defined it a thousand different ways) a modern business-focused characterization might be *"social capital is a set of various relationships, reputations, and assets, existing within an organization or with its partners and customers, that enable business processes to function as efficiently and effectively as possible."* Social capital is the value derived from positive connections between people. Connections breed trust and loyalty, powerful advantages in the business world. The proverbial "old pro", with a never-ending rolodex and friendly relationship with their clients' families, uses social capital as their primary tool for success.

Recently, scholars have started labelling two forms of social capital: bridging, or external connections between two groups; and bonding, or internal connections between people within the same group. Bridging might be a partnership between an advertiser and a sports team, and bonding might be a person's relationship with their co-workers. Both associations are based on social capital, but they change due to different actions. For instance, an entrepreneur isn't likely to attract business partners just because they refill the coffee pot where they work, but they might build bonding social capital with the people they work with.

As you may have noticed already, social capital is not a force confined to the financial world. Government institutions, politicians, businesses, communal clubs; everybody with a public image trades in social capital. Most lose social capital as well as build it; occasionally, at the hands of an enterprising journalist or because of a publicized disaster (think British Petroleum following the 2010 oil spill). More often, a person or business's social capital degrades because of incompetence or laziness.

Political scientist Robert Putnam, whom we will cover more thoroughly later, identifies the key benefit of social capital as reciprocity. That is, people or businesses doing things for one another because of a positive relationship. In his landmark book *Bowling Alone: The Collapse and Revival of American Community,* Putnam focuses on civic engagement as a reflection of a government's social capital with its citizens. Most notably, he identified declining voter turnout in presidential elections as a sign of the American government's problems maintaining social capital with their citizens, as well as support for foreign engagements. However, for now, we will maintain focus on the business sector, as that is where it is changing most rapidly.

To establish a clearer understanding of social capital, it is helpful to divide it into three main components: *relational capital, structural capital,* and *cognitive capital.*

Relational Capital

Most scholars agree that relational capital is paramount among the three divisions of social capital. It reaches the most people and encompasses the greater part of social capital's defined area, sometimes to the point of the two being used synonymously. However, the relational is made up purely of the behaviors that instill trust and respect within an organization and with its partners. Relational capital is responsible for most bridging behavior—forming good relationships with consumers and other entities—as well as some bonding within the company. Over time, as relationships are strengthened through consistent working interactions, relational capital between two people or organizations grows. These working associations aid in establishing collaborative processes which breed trust, loyalty, and growth as a team.

Building relational capital is, more than other forms of social capital, a habit. It comes from a long-time spent working with someone, fulfilling a role, and crafting an image as an individual or business that can be counted on. If you deliver good products consistently, you will win relational capital. When you are dealing with a person with whom you have built a great deal of relational capital, you probably have dealt with them many times, or, at least, built a good reputation before meeting them. The operative idea is dependability; a person who will always deliver results.

While all forms of social capital have a component centered on face-to-face interactions, relational capital relies on real-world communication most. Whether it's a business lunch between partners, or a salesman and their customer picking out a sundress at a fashion boutique, relational capital relies on more than a few emails or advertisements to grow.

By the same token, organizations lose relational capital through eliminating personal connections. More and more, meetings and partnerships are confined to the 1s and 0s of purely online interactions, and the classic "firm handshake, friendly smile" pitches are dismissed as an antiquated way of doing business. Owners have been moving away from time-tested tactics under the guise of swapping in cost-saving measures; after all, an email chain is free. Increasingly, second-rate technological substitutions are taking over the role of in-person meetings; and, while there are a few benefits in terms of convenience and spending, the detriment to relational capital is massive. Abandoning direct contact is a result of poor priorities, not frugality or technological savvy.

One common instance of relational capital being key is a person's choice where to get their hair cut. Whether it's a barber, hairdresser, or stylist; most people have a close relationship with the person who spends long periods of time around their head with a sharp pair of scissors. The average person goes to the same place for haircuts for many years, or even decades, and knows whoever is cutting their hair at least reasonably well. A huge part of this tightknit relationship is the extensive and intimate personal interaction built up over numerous visits. Trust and loyalty are there, not only because the barber does a good job, but because participants spend the entire transaction in one other's presence. It is relational capital that has numerous studies confirming people trust whoever is doing their hair. And it is relational capital that keeps people loyal to their barber or stylist after a trendier or cheaper spot has opened nearby. No consumers are scrambling for a fully-automated hair trimming experience, and that's because no "barber app" is ever going to build relational capital like an actual barber.

Structural and Cognitive Capital

Structural Capital is the next partition of social capital, and, of the three, it is the most static. Workers adapt to the structural capital inherent to their organization and business because it does not, and should not, change rapidly. Structural capital encompasses the processes, operational support structures, controls, and all functions that help people fill their roles within an organization.

It is crucial to facilitating the growth of bonding social capital. While bonding is, like most social capital, built on interpersonal relationships, good structural capital makes building those relationships easier. A company's on-boarding and training processes, both types of structural capital, can help a new person progress quickly in their role. The faster someone is proficient in their work, the more quickly they will be dependable and have a reputation as a person to count on. After that, it is simple enough to build relational capital.

While the human element of a business might shift, the framework of structural capital will endure. Over time, talented people or a fluctuating industrial environment can alter structural capital, but not with ease.

Cognitive capital is the force complimentary to structural capital. Simply put, cognitive capital is the skills, shared-norms, experience, and knowledge people possess, as well as an organization's trade secrets, patents, and market strategies. With each hiring or firing, a company's cognitive capital can change. Often, companies hire a person with high cognitive capital, as it is an incredibly important trait which is often predictive of a person's ability to do their job. A business looking for people with cognitive capital will often seek individuals with experience in the field or extensive education. Of course, cognitive capital also includes natural traits, such as inventiveness and the ability to cope with pressure. However, those are much more difficult to measure, and so tend to be neglected.

Structural capital creates a link between company processes and cognitive capital. It includes the tools people—and their accompanying cognitive capital—need to do their job. With limited structural capital, cognitive capital goes sorely underutilized.

Examples of structural capital that compliment cognitive capital are numerous. Many are methods or patterns the company employs to function, such as procedures for achieving a desired result, media for preparing employees to accomplish a goal, or some instances of intellectual property; IP that functions as a long-term aspect of company operations is structural, IP that is fluid and connected to a small group of individuals is cognitive.

One notable example, these days, is structural capital in the form of data sets. This is a somewhat more "exact" instance of social capital. However, like other types of structural capital, data sets act as instruments to enable company processes. Political campaigns have donor data and voter data they use to target their operations and coordinate volunteers (a form of cognitive capital). Advertisers target certain customers with consumer data. Big budget movies maintain massive databanks on audience preferences. The list goes on.

You may imagine, and rightly so, that this does not seem to fit with the narrative that social capital is decaying. If data is a part of structural capital and structural capital is a part of social capital, then it stands apart from companies' neglect of relational and cognitive capital. Intimate data sets on groups of people have never been more important. Every other week, tech companies are on the news for covertly mining and selling user data. Facebook may collapse if it continues its unrepentant exploitation of this opportunity.

However, after another look, you'll see this is exactly the point. Companies aren't just focusing on a specific element of their structural capital, namely the data they have collected, they are abusing it. Overuse, in this case, is the same as negligence. Whereas relational capital is dying a quiet death as business after business abandons face-to-face interactions in favor of impersonal high-tech substitutes, structural capital is being torn apart on center stage. Customers increasingly do not trust big business with their personal information and are taking steps to avoid manipulation. Entire companies are cropping up that exist just to help people guard against their personal info getting nicked.

Other forms of structural capital are decaying as well. Often, long held "ways of doing business" are being abandoned at a higher rate than ever. Relational capital, which acts as the external connection between companies and external agents, is decaying. As a result, structural capital and cognitive capital, the internal workings of a company, are rotting as well. Structural capital is having a problem just as surely as relational; it's just more noticeable. Put another way: it doesn't matter if your house collapses because of poor upkeep, or because someone sets it on fire, you'll still end up with nowhere to live.

For all this doom and gloom, there are some signs the negative trends of the last few decades are shifting. *Some* sectors of retail have started to recognize the importance of social capital, and change their business practices; certainly, for the better. However, we are getting ahead of ourselves. For now, let's explore the effects social capital can have on a business.

Chapter 2: Negative and Positive Social Capital

Of course, not all social capital is beneficial, or *positive*; often, it is poor, or *negative*. All the advantageous examples we explored in chapter one can have a potent effect in the opposite direction. Positive relational capital, a long-term trusting affiliation, can overcome a price disadvantage. However, a reputation for being inconsistent or uncaring counteracts lower prices in some instances.

This is clearest in the common difference between small retailers and big box stores: price vs. personality. Walmart might be cheap, but the mostly-faceless and detached corporation won't give customers the same level of on-hand attention a local business can. The battle between social capital and low cost is being fought in cities and towns across America, across nearly every type of business.

Positive Social Capital

A major way in which positive social capital affects modern business is by creating what has been dubbed by scholars: network reciprocity. In a reciprocal relationship, if you work with a vendor buying their products, they are more likely to do the same for you, or to refer you to other businesses they regularly work with. In *Reciprocity in Groups and the Limits to Social Capital*, Francis Bloch writes on the subject, "(reciprocal networks) are typically associated with norms that promote coordination, cooperation, and reciprocity for the mutual benefit of network members. The norms, coupled with the appropriate use of sanctions in case of non-compliance, are often thought to enable these groups to deal smoothly and effectively with multiple social and economic issues." People help each other when they are more strongly connected.

Knowledgeable business habits which build social capital will, over time, initiate a network of semi-interdependent businesses. This will lead to a series of direct and indirect benefits, including constancy from suppliers in the face of unfavorable market price fluctuations, streamlined business-to-business and customer interactions, and even allegiance against predatory competitors. All benefits here can come from internal practices to sustain and grow social capital.

Plainly, habits which create an intimate relationship with other people will have a huge upside. If a hardware store owner deals well with a carpenter over the course of months or years, that carpenter is likely to recommend the store to other carpenters, plumbers, or other small businesses in the trade community. In a strong relationship, outlets you are close to will even make a point of avoiding competitors to help you prosper.

Reciprocal relationships aren't the only major benefit of positive social capital; it will build customer loyalty as well. When customers see a business as charitable, high-quality, generous to employees, or any other trait that builds social capital, they will be more loyal. As with business relationships, customers prefer to buy their products from company's they feel good about. Whether that positive feeling comes from knowing their cashier, getting some more "human" experience than they would from another store, or just from the knowledge that the store gives to charity, people will respond to high social capital with regular patronage.

Do not underestimate the power of customer preference to overcome price. In 2014, the *Harvard Business Review* did a series of studies which attempted to quantify various aspects of social capital, specifically to understand their value in relation to competitive pricing. One survey had customers rate their service experience at various businesses on a scale of 1-10. Customers who reported a 9 or 10 spent 2.5 times as much money in an outlet annually as the average customer.

Negative Social Capital

As previously stated, it is also possible for businesses to attain negative social capital. They do this by consistently functioning with patterns of poor behavior; by being impersonal, inconsistent, or unethical. Persistent behaviors that turn off customers and shun relationships with suppliers and partners will hurt your social capital to the point where your reputation, relationships, and the basic structure of your company are harmful to the way you function.

Consciously or not, most business owners spend years, even decades, shaping the social capital of their company. What they value and the rules they enforce will add to or subtract from their social capital. People who push cheapness over customer satisfaction, competitiveness instead of a healthy reputation, and simplicity over personality, are generating negative social capital.

Crucially, while having poor social capital is undoubtedly bad for business, the practices that put you in a positive position may have a net positive effect. That is apparent in the many businesses today which make millions despite poor service, unfavorable public image, laughable business plans, or objectionable products.

McDonalds has raked in money for years by focusing on cheapness and speed. Their social capital is horrendous across most populations, but the cornerstones of their business model keep them afloat. It should be noted that McDonalds has taken major hits in North America—and good for us for rejecting a company which gets by on underestimating customers—but is staying strong overseas, especially in Asia, where many countries have accepted them, frozen burgers and all. Hopefully, the decline in the success of many low-quality fast food outlets is a sign of an uptick in social capital in the U.S., but other situations and numerous social scientists indicate the situation is still grave.

Negative social capital shows itself largely in the form of customer mistrust. When a company has a poor reputation; releases unattractive products, often a sign of poorly employed structural and cognitive capital; or doesn't pay enough attention to customers; it will earn suspicion. Customer mistrust means more resistance to price changes, greater willingness to switch to competitors, and lessened enthusiasm for new products or partners. When a target block of consumers believe a company's priorities don't match theirs, they might still do business with that company, but they will be on the lookout for an acceptable substitute.

Negative social capital is a powerful force for dissuading customer engagement. All businesses want, or at least should value, the people they do business with to be attentive to new company programs. When a professional baseball organization holds a team convention, they want their fans to show up. Having a fanbase that only purchases tickets for games will not maximize profit potential. To really make money, teams need to encourage their followers to buy jerseys and hats and other memorabilia. Groups of fans should be clamoring for tickets, driving up the cost of a seat, and devoting large parts of their lives to support players.

All of this comes from having positive social capital. It comes from cognitive capital, with a smart organization that has intelligent people and adept players trying to win. It comes from structural capital, with a team-wide philosophy centered around success. It comes from relational capital, with players and coaches who reach out to fans or sponsor charities. A focus on social capital in professional sport pays off on the team ledger. The proof is in the success of teams like the Chicago Cubs, New York Yankees, and Houston Astros, who followed the above tenets; and the failure of organizations like the Florida Marlins, who spent millions on a brilliant new stadium, but lost money because they neglected to promote a culture of winning, personality, or fan outreach.

Chapter 3: Measuring Social Capital

The one major weakness of social capital is how difficult it is to measure. Partially, this is due to its wide-range of definitions, but more so because this form of capital is based on relationships, not something which can be bought and sold. It is simple for everyone to understand when a person says, "I make $30,000 a year." However, "I have average social capital with two of my coworkers, but a lot of social capital with my boss," is far less universal. Even if the average business person had a clear understanding of social capital, those statements would mean different things to each listener.

People usually, scholars often, and economists especially, resist concepts that aren't reduced to a simple set of numbers. The lack of a universally-acknowledged quantifiable measure, a value that can sum up the worth of social capital, has plagued the field for years. Some, especially the more numbers-inclined experts, believe that social capital is not truly important if it cannot be calculated. And, while many mathematicians have attempted it; their efforts are not necessarily aimed at the average person. To explain why, I'll simply offer an example of a purposed function meant to be the starting point for Enrique Gonzalez-Aranguena, Anna Khmelnitskaya, Conrado Manuel, and Monica del Pozo's "Social Capital Index":

"A cooperative game with transferable utility (TU game) is a pair (N, v) where N = {1,...,n} is a finite set of n ≥ 2 players and v: 2N → IR is a characteristic function, defined on the power set of N, satisfying v(0/) = 0…The Shapley value [5] of a game v ∈ GN can be given by:"

$$\text{Shi}(v) = \sum T \subseteq N, T\ i\ \lambda v\ T, t \text{ , for all } i \in N,$$

If that information was useful to anyone, there are theorems, corollaries, and propositions on the subject to spare. However, this chapter is for more straightforward measurements that do not require advanced math to comprehend.

The most common approach to estimating the value of social capital is to combine the worth of the processes that it directly effects. While not perfect, it can be an extremely helpful method. Social capital is crucial because it improves outcomes for a business or person or institution, so a measurement based on the value of those results is intuitive.

Theory suggests that robust volunteer activity is the result of high social capital; more people donating their time for free means better relationships and reputation. Statisticians with the Office of Statistics for the United Kingdom wrote in their 2013 report, "Household Satellite Accounts— Valuing Volunteer Activity in the UK" that, "the value of frequent volunteer activity in the UK in 2012 was 1.5% of GDP. They continue to include that fluctuation in that percentage is directly connected to changes in the government's social capital.

Following a 2012 report from the Organization for Economic Cooperation and Development, the same organization developed a new, more comprehensive measure for a person's individual social capital based on a series of survey questions designed to address every aspect of all relationships in a person's life. The survey contained four parts, each focused on different sources of social capital: personal relationships, social network support, civic engagement, and trust and cooperative norms.

The questions on the survey came from numerous sources and ranged from, "Do you have at least one close friend?" to "Do you have a spouse, family member, or friend you can rely upon if you have a serious problem?" and "Have you been very involved in a political action in the last 12 months?". More yeses on these questions translate to a higher social capital score. While the organization behind this metric freely admits their collection of questions is not perfect, it is a straightforward idea that is easy to apply.

There have been other tries at creating a rubric to measure social capital in different contexts. In *The Role of Social Capital in Development: An Empirical Assessment,* Christian

Grootaert attempts to quantify social capital between settlements and the Indian government by evaluating local progress on a civics project: constructing regional watersheds. Grootaert cross-references a settlement's responses to survey questions regarding their relationship with the Indian government with the level of success they achieved building watersheds to estimate the value of social capital with an administration; what we might call *civic social capital*. However, while this attempt is certainly valid, the numerous variables at work confound the clarity of Grootaert's results. Social capital is clearly at play here, but the virtually limitless potential factors which go into producing a number measuring it make a result extremely hard to interpret. In short, his process is too specifically tailored to his subjects to translate to other people, organizations, or governments.

Throughout the years, there have been many other attempts to put a numerical value on social capital. But none have risen to universal recognition as superior or more effective. While those measures show promise, they still fall short of addressing a business reality. As such, *Understanding Social Capital 2.0* provides a tool to gain a unique understanding of your work environment as it gives you the ability to measure your "Social Capital Quotient" (SCQ). If your intelligence, which we measure with IQ, and personality come together to create the sum of you as a "whole person", then your SCQ shows the extent to which your "whole person" can influence those around you, specifically in the workplace.

While working in business, you are effectively able to measure your ability to lead, communicate with, and influence others by the strength of your relationships. The SCQ test can be taken at scqonline.us and the password for entry is SCQ2018. This will help you acquaint yourself with your current social capital status at work, and what you might do to improve it. A higher percentage indicates more robust social bonds with those around you. Focus on strengthening relationships with coworkers and understanding your role as a member of the team.

Chapter 4: Social Capital in Government

While we will spend most of this book focusing on the benefits of social capital as it pertains to business-customer relationships and coworker relationships, the large-scale effects social capital can have on a government are significant as well. A nation which has a government with high social capital and businesses who trend towards pursuing social capital will, without fail, be better off than countries who do not. Governments, especially presidential administrations, function better and exercise their agendas more effectively when they have high social capital. They are not especially different than businesses in this regard, with their citizens behaving the same way as customers would.

Looking through U.S. history, times of high social capital throughout society are invariably considered the country's greatest. When people feel engaged personally with their government and are closely-linked to the marketplace, prosperity abounds. There is no success without confidence and no affluence without trust. We grow the most and shed the least when disparate elements of humanity come together.

The most notable instance many people sight as a moment of greatness for the U.S. is our role in preventing a Nazi victory in World War 2. Stopping Hitler necessitated a massive unified effort from a democracy, something historically very difficult to achieve. However, that unification came, and America's greatest generation accomplished incredible things in the face of a terrifying opponent and dire consequences. The reason all of that was possible was because the government had social capital with its citizens.

If Robert Putnam wrote that civic engagement and trust in leadership was the sign of social capital in a country, America's effort in World War 2 is undeniably an example of that. Millions of Americans dropped their normal professions and abandoned people they loved to take part in the war effort. Social capital engenders customer retention in business, and it builds sustainable support from the populous in government. Great things are possible when a country has social capital. Normally indifferent parties put their back into a singular effort, and it sparks change.

What the country lacked in experience we made up for in resolve to defeat a foe far more prepared for battle than us. A quote from a German general following the war summed up our position succinctly, "One German-made Tiger Tank was worth four American-made Sherman Tanks. Unfortunately, the Americans always had five tanks." Countless lives were disrupted, and far too often extinguished. But people didn't give up on the cause; largely because they were led through the wilderness by leaders in government; foremost among them: President Franklin Roosevelt.

Roosevelt enforced extraordinary measures to mobilize all parts of the American economy and turn the country into a massive war machine. Under his direction, government workers flipped American culture upside down, not just through drafting and massive targeted spending, but through the most severe austerity regulations this country had ever experienced. A weaker government would have seen riots in every major city. However, with each iconic "fireside chat", Roosevelt smoothed over the nation's qualms with his actions, and maintained people's trust in his leadership.

All of this was possible because of social capital. In democracies, a government's social capital often matters more than the size of its war chest. If people don't have faith in their cause; reliance in the direction that their representatives are going, then all the money and power in the world won't carry the day. Social capital provides that focus, that interconnectedness; a citizen's belief that their actions will be reciprocated, in this case, by their government. Absent that, the best you can hope for is an ugly victory.

A Lack of Social Capital

Of course, this became very apparent several decades later when the U.S. stumbled into an ill-advised and not at all thought out war in Vietnam. There was no clear goal and no obvious entreaty; our enemy, the Vietcong, was not even the real enemy, that was the Soviet Union. Many soldiers fighting had little faith in the cause, and virtually no social capital with the government that sent them thousands of miles across an ocean to fight a war they didn't believe in. The U.S. had more bullets and bandages and thousands of tons of gear to equip troops, but the enemy had a clear motive to fight. The government had decreasing social capital with its people and army during this time, and no number of bombs or men could win it.

Adjusted for inflation, the U.S. spent well over a trillion dollars in the Vietnam war. While a sizable portion went to the air force and conducting massive bombing campaigns in North Vietnam, the government expended tremendous sums on equipment for ground forces. There are countless accounts of American troops, recently supplied for marches through the jungle, tossing their gear on the ground to make the trek easier, secure in the knowledge they would be fully restocked as soon as they reached another camp. Often, enemy forces would retrieve abandoned American equipment, so the U.S. ended up effectively arming their opponents. These are not the actions of people who believe in their leaders, or people who think their efforts will be reciprocated.

In the article "Social Capital and the Dynamics of Trust in Government" for the *American Journal of Political Science,* Luke Keele wrote, "From the late 1950s to the early 1970s, trust in government in the United States fell precipitously…it has been evident that citizens tend to generalize from recent government actions to form evaluations of government trustworthiness…Perhaps social capital is another broader process that underlies the movement of trust over time… a result of how much the public engages in civic life and the attendant attitudes of trust and reciprocity that develop in civic activity." There is arguably no more potent engagement in civic activity than serving in the nation's military. When that civic engagement began to look like a mistaken commitment, people turned on the government.

If the function of social capital is to use relationships to function as efficiently and effectively as possible, the U.S. government was working at a serious deficit. Had their level of social capital been higher, if the country was unified, the war would be won. However, the government pursued an unwise war, lost social capital with the populous, and were defeated.

Part Two: Roadblocks to Social Growth

Chapter 5: Basis of Social Capital Discrimination

When businesses focus on building social capital, it is largely beneficial to customers. When workers focus on building social capital, it is generally positive for the health, efficiency, and connectivity of a workplace. However, vast accumulation of social capital, like the vast accumulation of wealth, leads to rising inequality in holding social capital, and that can be detrimental to almost everyone involved.

It is a simple fact that, in a closed system like a business, there is a finite amount of social capital to go around. Levels of social capital induce the production of a ranking system among employee relationships. If trust is a good indicator of social capital standing, which all empirical markers show is true, and most scholars believe to be the case, then it follows that people will naturally, if unconsciously rank their fellow employees, subordinates, and bosses based on the strength of social bonds formed. Everyone has people they prefer to work with; people they count on more than others to carry out a task. This is the result of engrained social capital, and while it is not inherently bad, too great a disparity in social capital can create problems.

Biases

The nature of peoples' relationship-building process is fundamentally flawed. We depend on biases, whether we want to or not, to decide whom we trust the most. Biases are a kind of shortcut, a simple way to decide something rapidly. Instead of spending a long time gathering a great deal of information, we use biases to draw conclusions based on limited evidence. Bias has a bad reputation because it is the basis for negative stereotypes, but bias is, at its core, just a decision-making tool founded on perceived patterns. Whether those perceptions are fair or moral dictates the ethics of the resulting bias. Unfortunately, we are frequently unaware of our biases, and need to make an effort to identify and control them once formed.

Often, we are simply biased towards people who are most similar to us. People who look like us, who enjoy the same things as us, who share basic traits with us. It is completely human to trend towards favoring people in that way. We bond over commonalities, not differences. If we choose superficial commonalities, if we act on unfair biases, our decisions are damaging. But, in the workplace, if we choose the right commonalities to bond over, such as a zeal for high-quality performance or, at least, similar difficult job experiences, the bonds we form are healthy and will build stronger and more beneficial relationships.

This is all building to a simple truth: antiquated long-term social capital can lead to discrimination and responsible members of society should work hard to root it out wherever possible. When the moral compasses of social capital leaders in a company, industry or government have ossified, they cannot be allowed to remain so frozen. Often couched under the guise of "tradition", unfair social capital build-up in the proverbial old guard brings progress to a standstill and engenders discrimination at every turn. Notions about a particular way of behaving, completing a task or falling into the trap of "this is the way we've always done it," must be avoided.

Doing things the way they have always been done, relying on people who know the fundamentals of business, not rocking the boat; these are all synonyms for refusing change and ignoring people who don't fit a certain mold. Whether that is keeping down people on the basis of how they look or how they were raised, or how well or poorly they have been educated, the social capital of people at the top too often determines how people at the bottom rise.

It would be a mistake to continue the conference on social capital without covering the effects and history of race, gender, class, and any other differentiating status on gathering, maintaining, and using social capital. While the mechanisms of social capital work similarly for, for instance, a lower-class male/female from rural communities or upper-class male/female from urban centers, it is undeniable that the two people will have a different experience with social capital by dint of their traits. They face different biases and operate in different circles with unequal access to the levers of power in society.

This is not to say that all such cases of biased inclusion are malicious. As previously stated, people generally gravitate towards others who are similar through no fault of their own. Humans trend towards sameness. It's easy to make relationships that way. Far from patterns as nasty as racism or socioeconomic class discrimination, these biases can be anodyne. If a common interest in baseball bolsters an employee's bond with a boss, ultimately leading to more attention and eventually a promotion, that isn't sinister. It is, however, damaging and unfair, and organizations should be doing everything they can to combat it. Consider that certain groups of people may not like baseball, and that reflexive draw towards someone who does acts as a blinder to otherwise-qualified workers. At least at work, we have to be civilized enough to judge people on only the most prescient qualities, who has the best skillset for the job or else we risk a great deal.

Recognition

The effort involved in instituting this inequality is often not an instinct. Monitoring and controlling a natural tendency requires sustained exertion. However, purposeful deviation towards equality cannot be viewed as a unique virtue, rather as a necessity and prerequisite for moral rectitude. If we acknowledge that most people grow some level of negative bias over the course of their lives, and further we accept that, for the betterment of everyone, those biases should consciously be overturned, it does no good to herald an unbiased person as exceptional.

To put it simply: everyone has negative biases about other people. And we all need to work against those biases. This is especially true when it comes to social capital, where close relationships, and especially trust, are the currency. No one is owed a trophy for not acting on their problematic biases. Rather, people who are too sluggish or in denial about reality deserve a rebuke. High fives for doing what should be expected don't help. They make doing the right thing stand out and set back the movement towards equality and fairness.

Chapter 6: Types of Discrimination

Social capital discrimination occurs in two significant patterns: relational discrimination, in which people form robust positive relationships with others based on bias; and structural discrimination, in which the underlying apparatus of a society, business, or government favors certain groups with trust and other benefits of social capital more than others. The two come from the same unfortunate tendencies people have; that is, acting on unfair biases built on limited or skewed observations. However, one is much more difficult and overreaching than another to get rid of.

Relational Discrimination

First, Relational discrimination is an individual problem. Every person needs to deal with it on their own and attempt to police that wrong when they see it in others. If you pay attention to your actions and look for your biases, it's not easy, but you can correct your course. For instance, a common issue is approaching those who aren't well-educated with condescension and dismissing their ideas as if a degree was necessary to have an intelligent conversation. A simple fix for this is to not do it. While that might sound pithy or reductive, the fact is that, while you aren't in total control of your biases, you are in charge of your actions. A bias not acted on isn't much of a problem—and should ultimately go away.

Checking this behavior is especially important for people in positions of power. Those in the upper echelons of social circles or businesses or at the controlling levels of government are trendsetters. If the "higher-ups" reject certain biases, others will follow; and if they give in to and embrace those biases, that can have great influence as well. Bosses can set a tone for their employees. They show what behavior is acceptable, and what is rewarded. They can also make it clear what is a detriment to a person's chances of success. If leadership does not tolerate or act upon bigotry in their relationships, it will be less likely to occur among rank and file employees.

Structural Discrimination

The second form of social capital discrimination is structural, and it is much more difficult to eradicate than simple instances of relational discrimination. As it is with the differences between relational and structural capital, the associated discrimination patterns are not equal. Structural social capital is built into the foundations of company processes and it effects employees and customers alike.

Our previous definition of structural capital was capital that "encompasses the processes, operational support structures, controls, and all functions that help people fill their roles within an organization." Logically, a discriminative toxic company structure uses those processes, support structures, and various basic functions to aid certain groups more than others. This partiality leads to unequal resource allocation, such as not enough workers being assigned to a project with a female manager; insufficient support structures, such as the highly-educated not receiving fair priority with technical support staff; or a habitual indifference to the contributions of minority employees on managerial levels. All these are functions of structural discrimination, and they occur constantly.

That ties-in direction to another trademark of healthy structural capital: the ability to identify, implement, and reward cognitive capital. A company's structure is comprised of the tools and systems necessary for smart people to effectively do their work. However, what happens when that structure turns discriminatory? Its purpose is reversed. Instead of even and efficient resource allocation for workers, the company will have unequal capital flow and extreme preference; which will, in turn, create chaos or, at least, negligence. If structural capital enables cognitive capital, structural discrimination disables it. Good minds go to waste, and less-qualified or capable individuals get too much credit. All the cognitive capital in the world can be negated by structural discrimination in a business.

Too often, foundations of business culture, often formed in rashly different times, were born in a society that not only accepted, but encouraged some form of discrimination; in some cases, actively profiting by it. While those attitudes are beginning to crumble under the assault of a long-fought war of attrition, they are certainly still evident in businesses everywhere. Maybe muted, but surely sustained.

Prejudice in Government

This is certainly evident in government as well as business. In "Individual Level Evidence for the Causes and Consequences of Social Capital", John Brehm and Wendy Rahn follow the Robert Putnam assertion that social capital in government can manifest as civic engagement from citizens. "In our structural model, we posit that people who trust others have greater confidence in political institutions…Such compliance is of fundamental importance for the state, because it means that political authorities have less need to rely upon heavy-handed enforcement and politically expensive coercion to control citizens' behavior." It follows that unequal trends in civic engagement in relational groups signify unequal levels of a government's social capital. The government's implementation of its own practices works somewhat differently than a business's with regard to structural capital. However, the two are different institutions with varying goals.

Arguably, structural capital for a government includes its laws and legislative agenda. They are the processes by which they facilitate their plans. The government's purview is its country, and its cognitive capital is therefore its citizens. If a major factor for determining structural capital is how efficiently and fairly it controls cognitive capital, then laws are unquestionably a tool for that purpose.

Therefore, structural discrimination for a government includes discriminatory laws. Laws which promote racism, sexism, or classism. That bias understandably lowers the government's social capital with those groups. Social capital being one of the most crucial aspects to winning an election, politicos who are interested in remaining in power should focus on growing their social capital with the electorate.

Steven Knack clarifies this in his book *Social Capital and Government: Evidence from the United States*. "Social capital—in the form of general trust and strong civic norms that call

for cooperation when large-scale collective action is need—
can improve government performance in three ways: It can
broaden government accountability, making government
responsive to citizens at large rather than to narrow
interests. It can facilitate agreement where political
preferences are polarized. It is associated with greater
innovation when policymakers face new challenges." A
government's lack of structural discrimination is not only
beneficial to government operations and agendas, but to
the interpersonal dealings of those within the government's
grasp. When groups are polarized and neither trusts their
government due to perceived bias, chaos is an inevitable
result. Arguably, that is the modern condition.

Results of Discriminatory Behavior

A lack of structural discrimination is good for everybody.
People have numerous roles in society, and whether you
are in power, in government, a leader in business, an
employee, or a voter, structural discrimination won't be
good for you. The disintegration of cognitive capital makes
businesses weaker, the invitation for chaos destabilizes the

country; negative biases inhibit the best of society's role-players from fulfilling their duty properly, and responsible people must work hard to eliminate them.

Of course, structural bias, being by necessity, hard to change, will take a great effort *en masse* to fix. We have to examine the underlying processes we use to conduct business. Leaders will have to devote time to study if certain practices, especially those that have been in place for a long time, are skewing the playing field for some members of the work force. Statistical analysis can play a significant role in this switch. Finding patterns is the key to solving this problem and producing a fairer world for everyone.

Chapter 7: Minority Status

Of the various major forms of social capital discrimination, unfair treatment on the basis of race is one of the most notable. To state the obvious, a person's racial appearance or genuine heritage significantly affects how some people treat them. This stems from centuries of socially structuralized bias, the history of which could fill numerous volumes, and has, of course, been studied at great length by scholars around the globe.

However, for our purposes, the coverage of far-reaching effects of historical inequality will remain confined to the topic of social capital. Our society is a melting pot of different cultures. The built-in potential for racial discrimination that is present in operational and social structures exists due to the culmination of immigration spanning hundreds of years. All the good that structural capital can do within a business brings problems when that structure is infused with racial animus. And while structural problems have the deepest roots, relational and cognitive capital are doled out on similarly uneven scales.

Segregation and "Raced Spaces"

The history of racism in America primarily traces back to the ethnic clashes between Europeans and Native Americans. However, it would be misleading to say that the nature of those relationships were due to something as small as a lack of social capital, or anything approaching that. They were atrocities, and socioeconomic forces such as social capital don't apply.

Following the death of slavery and the conclusion of major hostilities between settlers and Native Americans, social capital became a recognizable force. Surely, the birth of Jim Crow laws and growth of legally protected racism in America was just as much about preventing African Americans from accruing social capital as it was keeping them impoverished, unable to vote, and uneducated. A system we unfortunately still see in place today due to structuralized welfare which has been promoted by the Democratic party. If the term had been coined a hundred years earlier, there would be volumes of documents by powerful bureaucrats explicitly stating the need to keep minorities from gaining social capital, as there are with the other three conditions.

If, as many historians contend, the purpose of Jim Crow laws were to limit African American ascension in America following a relatively peaceful period during early reconstruction, then the ability to forge social capital was a necessary target for those laws. Relational social capital was and is a generational commodity for individuals and families. Having close ties to influential people can make a career for a parent, their children, and even grandchildren, if the relationship is well-tended. Minorities and those of lower socio-economic standing attaining social capital with those in power would be a major blow to people who were working to keep them as subjugated as possible.

Segregation was one of the main results of this effort. While racial disdain was, of course, a central driver pushing segregation in many laws, forced separation also had the desired effect of distancing African Americans from powerful people. If the two races were separate, any potential social capital building between blacks and most of the white ruling class was cut off. Within African American communities, social capital building continued at a normal pace. However, that was mostly bonding capital; or intercommunal connections with other blacks, where bridging capital, in this case connections between racial groups, would have much more power and utility.

Of course, at the federal level, the Supreme Court infamously ruled in favor of "Separate but equal" practices in Plessy v Ferguson. However, the laws which enforced segregation were largely imposed by individual states, so there are quite a few to choose from. They often came in the form of many states' "Black Codes", which codified a few African American civil rights, but mostly made practices that would allow them to rise economically illegal and kept African Americans apart from higher society as much as possible.

In "The Legal Creation of Raced Space: The Subtle and Ongoing Discrimination Created Through Jim Crow Laws", Frances Edwards and Grayson Thompson write about the late 19th century laws which laid the foundation for a divided America; a country in which social capital would remain divided by race. "Jim Crow Laws codified discriminatory practices and provided the legal framework necessary for the unequal treatment of African Americans. This inequality was pervasive and extended to the way individuals lived and functioned within society…These laws intentionally, yet subtly, created a kind of 'raced space.'" Edwards and Thompson go on to enumerate how "raced spaces" essentially created single-race subcommunities in America.

By limiting interactions between the upper class, who held most political and economic power over the country, minorities and those with low socio-economic standing had little to no opportunity to build trust and engender reciprocity with those in power. And without being able to take part in organizational structures, those raced spaces ensured that important structural capital grew without contributions from these communities. This separation is largely why the business world is taking so long to accommodate all races. Many institutions bear structural capital founded in racially homogeneous conditions.

Evolution of Race-Based Laws

The long and sordid history of anti-racial laws did not stop in America, nor were they confined to African Americans. Legislation to limit the rights of immigrants from countries ranging from Ireland and Italy; to Japan; to Mexico; to most recently, Syria, Iran, and others; has been inflicted on people. Often, this comes clothed in notions regarding the security of American culture. However, in most cases, these orders are about limiting social capital growth. While literal bans on monetary gain are less common, continuing pseudo-segregation practices, echoes of past Jim Crow laws, and protections for the ruling class's virtual monopoly on social capital attainment are much easier to get away with.

While legal segregation is far less pervasive, its effects are still potent. In "Race, Gender, and the Invisible Hand of Social Capital", Steve McDonald and Jacob Day study the lingering effects of segregation, how it depresses social capital achievement, and the impact that suppression has on race and gender. "(The power of social capital) is best illustrated by recent research that focuses on how high-level positions are often filled by workers who do not search for their jobs (McDonald 2008; McDonald and Elder 2006). These 'non-searchers' receive unsolicited job information that leads to employment in some of the best jobs around. This informal recruitment process is also more effective for men and women of higher socio-economic status than for men and women of lower socio-economic standing, demonstrating how the 'invisible hand' of social capital helps to maintain certain inequality." Social capital, in this case, leads to informal connections to people in charge of powerful and lucrative job positions. These informal connections are an extremely effective tool which can directly lead to less-qualified candidates being hired. Truly, Jim Crow's hold over social capital is not over.

Notes on Personal Appearance

Racial animus has roots inherent to ethnicity. However, often aggressors simply determined that by appearance, and people who do not fit the persecuted heritage receive the same prejudice nonetheless. In the gender studies journal *Gender and Society*, Margaret Hunter published an examination titled "'If You're Light You're Alright': Light Skin Color As Social Capital for Women of Color". Hunter finds distinct correlations between skin tone and educational achievement, spousal status, and income. "Skin color stratification, differentiation by light or darkness of skin tone, continues to be a significant sociological issue in both the African American and the Mexican American communities today…I contend that light skin works as a form of social capital for women. In this case, light skin is interpreted as beauty, and beauty operates as social capital for women. Women who possess this form of capital are able to convert into economic capital, educational capital, or another form of social capital." If beauty can be used to forge stronger relationships and influence relational connections to a greater degree, it is a form of currency, especially for women.

That alone is far from ideal, especially in a traditional workplace where good looks often have little to do with job effectiveness. Combined with societal bias towards women of light skin and against women of dark skin, these inclinations become an extremely potent negative force. However, we are straying into issues of gender, which are due their own chapter.

Chapter 8: Gender Discrimination

Not unlike racism and socio-economic discrimination, sexism has a long history of impacting peoples' ability to gather social capital. Also, like racism, the suppression of women's rights was done largely in an effort for those in authority to maintain a monopoly on power, including the maintenance and exchange of high-level social capital. However, there are key differences between the two. First, minorities faced a concentrated subjugation from whites throughout all levels of society as well as elected officials which can be easily pinpointed on a timeline of legislative efforts, as well as major changes, both positive and negative, in statistics on acts of violence. Women have faced a more generalized oppression with the major turning points mostly being victories for feminist movements, and not overt policy and behavioral changes by misogynists.

Second, African Americans, on some occasions due to their acting to achieve some distinction of higher status and others simply when faced with bad luck, were lynched. While women faced violence in many aspects of life, as well as consistent sexual oppression which did not affect black men to the same degree, ritualistic mob actions were not a threat to their realizing more rights and the ability to tenure social capital in influential positions.

These major differences signify two different agendas on the part of persecutors. It is useless to parse what motivations lay in the hearts of perpetrators. However, the paths of these two groups were certainly difficult as they struggled for equality. McDonald and Day wrote on the two journeys, "…gender differences may be because of women knowing people in fewer occupations than men (Campbell 1988) and their heavier reliance on strong ties such as close friends and family members (Ibarra 1997; Moore 1990; Smith 2000). Racial and ethnic minorities also tend to be cut off from personal and professional connections and have low levels of opportunity in general that leads to worse outcomes when in search of social capital (Mouw 2002; Parks-Yancy 2006)." Again, as with ethnic minorities, women suffer from a lack of bridging social capital, and are forced to rely heavily on bonding capital to make up for that.

While women never faced a formal segregation effort, they did fight for the vote. As discussed, voting is a key component in a government's move to secure social capital with its constituents. The fact that women could not vote for so many years speaks to a fundamental deficiency in the government's structural capital. Given that the government had such a kneejerk disdain for their contributions, it is even more startling the level of civic engagement that suffragists like Susan B. Anthony and Elizabeth Stanton displayed with their efforts to take part in the electoral process. Faith in the capabilities of a government which is categorically rejecting your abilities based on selfish reasons requires an uncommonly long-term outlook.

In Modern Business

Despite advances in women's rights movements, modern company culture almost always includes discrimination of some kind, malicious or otherwise. Not all discrimination comes from a place of malice or even conscious action. Much of the negative bias is engrained behavior a male-friendly world has taught people to believe. However, conscious or not, hateful or not, discrimination does damage, and is harming women in workplaces across America.

Sharon Timberlake, in her study "Social Capital and Gender in the Workplace", found that "Although the numbers of women entering the workplace have risen steadily in the last half century and strides have been made in attaining economic parity with men, statistics reveal that women continue to lag behind men in career advancement and in levels of compensation and achieved status. It is argued in the literature that women are hindered in their efforts to achieve career advancement and its associated benefits due to their inability to access social capital, a valuable organizational commodity and source of the knowledge, resources, and networks that are essential for career development and maturation." While women are attaining higher education more than ever, and achieving full-time employment at record rates, they often lack the necessary connections with fellow employees and managerial personnel to advance to upper management.

This is not due to a natural deficiency of any kind, but with a fault in the formation of society. Men are conditioned by an unfair system to reject women out of hand, and, due to a lack of consciousness regarding this privilege, not subject to change themselves or call out others. While it is, understandably, difficult for someone to admit they had a leg up over some of their competition, as this somewhat diminishes the height of their accomplishments, that is the case. Until more men begin to realize the problem and act to squash this inequality, our tilted system is destined to remain static.

"Gendered Spaces"

In the previous chapter we discussed the problem of "raced spaces". They are divisions between ethnic groups, in America especially blacks and whites, that are leftover relics of segregation laws as well as other racially-motivated socioeconomic forces. The same spaces exist as a division between men and women, and, like their racial counterparts, they cause significant trouble and inequality in the ability to gather social capital at higher levels of social strata.

"Gendered spaces" are generated and enforced by society-wide ideas of the varying roles of women and men. While the years are eroding at those notions, chipping away at old stereotypes; prejudice still, of course, is a very powerful motivator. For instance, despite countless instances of astounding female athletic achievements, sports are still an area dominated by men. There is no component of athletic interest coded into a Y chromosome, there is no natural law that governs who likes what. However, too often, sports are exclusionary areas for women of all ages, and many girls are raised, overtly or otherwise, with the lesson that men are the only "real athletes".

This idea is forged in ignorance. Separation of male and female athletes makes sense in some cases, as certain skill differences are irreconcilable in some areas. However, great female competitors abound. Hall of Fame softball pitcher Jenny Finch was one of the most dominant athletes of her generation and put on numerous displays in which she struck out groups of professional male hitters. Simone Biles has piled up stunning performances in international gymnastics where she is a paramount competitor. Of course, there could be a whole debate about the undeniable success, yet underpayment of the worlds professional female soccer teams. Perhaps most shockingly (to some), powerlifter BeccaSwanson squatted 843 pounds, outpacing every NFL team weight room record by a wide margin. The point is, female athletes accomplish astounding feats regularly. However, women are still often left out of the world of athletics.

Exclusion like this, with little basis in realty, is clearly another attempt to keep power in traditionally male institutions. While sports do not hold any official sway, like the government, where women are also underrepresented, they are a potent force within society, both economically and culturally. By keeping this space largely male-run, an important access point for social capital is cut off. People build relationships around, in some cases, their mutual interests. Sports being a common interest for many people, keeping athletics a male-dominated area is keeping a tool for social capital solely for men.

Sports are hardly the only gendered space within American society. Male culture is assigned control over a wide-range of social areas, especially those involving advanced education and intelligence, most notably engineering. While there are still generations of girls who want to grow up to be inventors and scientists and doctors, often there are subtle and sometimes not-so-subtle nudges for them to deviate towards a more "traditionally female" goal.

This prodding, sometimes on the part of parents, teachers, classmates, or any number of major role-players in a woman's life, takes perfectly capable and potentially fantastic female professionals and point them towards a less-powerful or influential, neutral or female gendered space. To be clear, while male gendered spaces are the preeminent cause of gender inequality, there are non-gendered spaces—medicine is increasingly moving in that direction—as well as some female gendered spaces where men face some degree of exclusion themselves. The fashion industry is one lucrative example where men find themselves at a disadvantage in terms of gathering social capital simply by nature of their gender.

Gender social capital disparity and gendered spaces need to become relics of the past. They divide people unfairly and they cut off potentially brilliant and groundbreaking individuals from doing what would serve society best. America cannot stand the failing of living by past prejudices planted in a time when men laid claim to every available lever of power. The best of us will continue to fight for a time when opportunities, including those for social capital, will be completely equal. Unfortunately, while gender and ethnicity are the largest impediments to fairness in this country, they are not the only powerful prejudices governing the success or failure of numerous Americans.

Chapter 9: Bias on Socioeconomic Status

Another major and unfair detriment to social capital acquisition is a person's socioeconomic position. Despite America being the "land of opportunity", a lack of economic resources is as sure a way as any to keep a person from attaining a high position in society. The same walling off that raced and gendered spaces create, the same prevention from contact with social capital-vested individuals, is present when someone doesn't have enough money.

Of course, upper- and lower-income groups travel in different circles. This begins with housing. Rich people live in more expensive homes in neighborhoods with high property values. Low-income families do not. Wealthy kids attend more expensive private schools and there they grow the social barriers which keep them apart from lower-income kids, for whom the same is true with public schools. Going to college can be a somewhat equalizing experience, as poor kids can make it to more expensive universities through athletic or academic merit, and upper-class kids might choose a cheaper university for several reasons.

However, by that point, young adults have mostly solidified their social attitudes regarding people of different socioeconomic distinctions into life-long thought patterns and behavior tendencies; ways of thinking that are difficult to overcome. While some people can get over negative stereotypes, plenty cannot, and social barriers, which before were enforced by parental choices and other involuntary circumstances, become a fully-artificial blockade to the pursuit of equal social capital flow. These are further enforced by superficial differences, like who can wear expensive clothes or go to high-end restaurants, which make non-practical situations skew heavily towards the well-off.

While this might, on the surface, appear like a milder prejudice which could create little more than differing political ideologies, that is a massive underestimate of the value of spending recreational time with someone in a power position. Getting drinks or going to a basketball game can overcome hours of hard-work when it comes to building social capital. Connections built at a concert can endure quite a bit, and soporific power point presentations don't help a person's case nearly as quick as a few rounds of golf. Without the ability make connections like that, people with less money will always have a harder time dealing social capital, regardless of talent or personality.

In "Social Capital, Socioeconomic Status and Self-efficacy", Jing Han, Xiaoyuan Chu, Huicun Song, and Yuan Li, made the case for social capital being a tool for maximizing a person's abilities; a modifier which could power middling workers to the top or chain exceptional employees to moderate success. Besides another robust attempt to quantify social capital—"$SC = \beta_0\ \lambda_5 SES + \lambda\ \Sigma \lambda_6 CV + \varepsilon$"—the researchers offer these insights as two of the results of their study, "(2) There is a significant positive correlation between the family socio-economic status as well as all its dimensions and self-efficacy; the socioeconomic status, with its dimensions, is the predictive variable of self-efficacy…(4)Social capital plays a significant intermediate role between socio-economic status and self-efficacy, and the mediating effect size is about 51.75%." In plainer language, where someone begins economically, specifically their immediate family's surroundings, determines how successful they are later in life. This is true largely because social capital, which is closely-tied to socioeconomic status, makes someone more effective in a competitive area, especially when it comes to making money. Social capital enables those who have it to achieve more, and hurts many who don't possess it, stopping them from realizing their goals.

These are the most direct results of poor economic standing. Of course, the vast web of indirect effects of a poor upbringing is almost too large to contemplate, and sociologists spend careers trying to decipher the true causes of a problem. A lack of money is often strongly correlated to poor health, partially due to less-nutritious food, partially due to lower levels of medical care. The same goes for educational achievement, potentially because of absent parents, less engagement in extracurricular activities, or a carryover from health problems. Criminality is also an issue, as is drug abuse. Most of these problems are similarly reversed with a middle to upper class upbringing (although not in every case, of course), and they generally lead to social capital problems as well. Prejudice of nearly every sort exists against these conditions, and it acts to stunt relationships and slow the growth of trust.

Roots of U.S. Bias

It would be remiss to exclude the origins of socioeconomic bias in America. Certainly, this bias is common to most world cultures to a degree that other negative biases, such as ethnic prejudice, are not. The roots of this harmful outlook stem from early American ideals about class that sprung from British heritage customs. Imitating the social layering patterns of the aristocracy was natural behavior. The wealthy set social agendas and power brokered, and those with less scrambled to behave similarly. Powdered wigs and frock coats aside, money always means power, and powerful set the tone for their contemporaries.

Even when the Brits fell out of favor with most people and ultimately fell or fled during the revolution, and the most "blatantly English" customs were unpopular, people who had land or other property they gained during British rule remained on top. As George Washington's diary entries on physical etiquette when first meeting someone and Thomas Jefferson's letters regarding cutlery placement at the dining room table prove, the founding fathers, until they decided to scribble down several "self-evident truths" were generally models of British gallantry. The conclusion of the American Revolutionary War at the colonies' victory at Yorktown did not alter the class system in the newly-formed United States immediately, and we are left dealing with the remnants of said system still.

These leftovers were the foundation of numerous toxic structural capital networks. People stuck with people based on elite memberships in institutions where entry was concerned largely with lineage. Parents passed down the best opportunities to the most accredited academic institutions or exclusive social clubs to their sons and daughters, and people without a family connection were shut out. The heart of elitism lays in family connections like this; where structural capital is a person's birthright, as opposed to a system based on personal merit or serving the common good.

And elitism ties in perfectly to racism, socio-economic discrimination and discrimination based on gender. Members of the social aristocracy have protected their own for centuries, and, apart from schools and influential community institutions, this protection extended to major businesses and titans of industry that shaped the American economy. Having money or at least a "proper upbringing" gave someone the access points for building social capital with people who counted. It provided another barrier for those who did not.

Bias manifests in a variety of different ways. In many situations, and, as far as the founders would most likely be of the opinion, a lacking of higher education works against someone. Whether it's a job interview, a date, or simple conversion with someone you've just met, lacking advanced education can be a significant detriment to a person's opportunities to make personal connections and cultivate social capital.

Chapter 10: Educational Bias

Socioeconomic biases have similar carryovers to bias based on educational status as well. Many employers will regard degrees in much higher esteem than what is reasonable compared to experience and aptitude. A person's ability to perform their job adequately is certainly difficult to assess before they begin working and focusing on education can provide a shortcut to estimating their quality. However, that focus often leads to an unfair degree of favoritism. People who can't boast advanced instruction get left behind.

In "Social Capital in Action: Alignment of Parental Support in Adolescents' Transition to Postsecondary Education", Doo Whan Kim and Barbara Schneider explores the connection between parents' social capital and their children's acceptance into selective higher-education institutions. "Through actions that are functionally specific to (an) adolescent's goal of gaining admission to college, parents can provide a bridge to resources and information outside the family that enable the adolescent to make a more informed choice of college; such actions reflect parents' dynamic role as social resources for their children. In particular, we pay attention to different social support options that parents can activate for their adolescents depending on their socioeconomic status." Essentially, a parent's job becomes much more difficult and their options greatly limited if they don't have enough money to provide their kid with resources to succeed and make it into a good college. Parents must be very involved in their children's lives to make up for the lack of resources elsewhere. However, that is not always possible, and even if it is, children are stuck in a space without access to bridging social capital opportunities.

Caregivers without money, resources, or helpful connections need to make up for that with personal contributions of time. This helps build close familial ties, strengthening relational capital, and, according to several major scholars you will discover later on, powerful family bonds can approach the strength of a more professional and traditional work network, at least when it comes to the issue of support. Kim and Schneider again: "Academic help, proper guidance for school programs and information about the college admissions process, and institutional agents in the school can provide strong network ties that compensate for family networks when students' parents have limited economic and social resources. A positive social relationship between parents/children and these resource- providers becomes important in expanding the scope of available resources to secure better educational and occupational opportunities later in life."

However, despite the potential lower-income families have to equalize the potential relational and cognitive capital gains that money can provide, structural capital remains centered to benefit a relatively small group of people, many of whom have close relational ties as well. The foundations of major social and business institutions are tied to specific groups, and everyone else has to manage that disadvantage when they are working for social capital. Unfortunately for the well-educated, and others who have risen to levels of academic distinction, there are certain competitive sectors where hard-won traits actually hold people back, and these areas compose significant impediments to certain people's advancement in life.

Abnormal Company Cultures

Some companies attempt to create an anti-establishment, "anti-indoctrination", or simply anti-norm culture, and use that as justification to suppress or push out the educated and the well-versed. Valuing practical experience, and people who have not been shaped by another potentially damaging culture, can have benefits. Truly, experience and recommendations are valuable information when it comes to confirming a person's quality; they should not be overlooked. But when any kind of attachment to a "normative" process, such as an advanced degree, is looked upon as problematic, then management have most-likely overcorrected. Despite selection bias, prime institutions, such as post-graduate study programs, still convey significant expertise and generally train excellent students.

After understanding major negative biases that pervade mainstream business, the growth of anti-establishment culture makes sense. But, when taken to extremes, it drives away talented individuals and is detrimental. The movement against learning is apparent in numerous big businesses. If a fully-qualified employee, working in an unconventional and anti-education-facing field, such as hardware or mechanics, faces a ceiling on his or her progress in a career, simply because they took a traditional route and achieved academic standing, that company is under misguided leadership.

Hopefully, problems such as extreme anti-establishment direction can self-correct. It is a harmful course that will hurt many businesses' bottom lines. More important, streaks of over-independence are not as engrained in structural capital as ethnic prejudices or misogyny. However, it is still crucial to call them out when apparent. After all, they are yet another manifestation of negative bias which infects modern life.

Chapter 11: Attempts to Solve Prejudice

It has long been clear that there are no easy solutions to problems of institutionalized bias. Leaving it untended and hoping it fixes itself is unrealistic. While various legal actions have slowly moved the ball forward, progress is achieved at a glacial pace. Society is nearly always in a "one step forward, one and a half steps back" mode. America perpetually bounds from one extreme to another; from growth to decay, and from buoyancy to nihilism.

As the years pass, attempts at solutions as well as natural ameliorating forces have cropped up. Human efforts to impose equality and fairness have been met with varying degrees of success and require a great deal of effort to implement. Whether these answers come in the form of courtroom decisions or social movements, they have not provided more than a semblance of equality, and often not even that. Organic solvents are becoming more powerful, and in those, the key to fixing social capital inequality might lay.

Business Fixes

We can briefly touch on some widely-accepted notions that are not overly contentious to most and have made inroads against society-wide social capital inequalities, even in structural capital, that most difficult of areas. A proactive company culture leadership must be alert for the possible pitfalls of engrained social capital. Self-awareness is the key to fighting against accidental bias. Knowledge of our own tendencies and potential for partiality will help us avoid it. When people in positions of privilege are blind to their situation, biases do the most damage. Those who are asleep at the wheel or outright deny the possibility of problems often do the most damage.

Another attempt, aside from proactive changes to personal behavior and company cultures, to lessen racial and gender-based discrimination is affirmative action. The notion is that if African American students, especially in the case of affirmative action, are given some degree of preference during selection for higher institutions, especially college, that will offset disadvantages based on society-wide racist trends as well as socioeconomic disadvantages which remain resulting from slavery. There are *volumes* of data outlining the success or failure, fairness or inequality, and feasibility or impossibility of different versions of affirmative action.

In "Best Practices or Best Guesses? Assessing the Efficacy of Corporate Affirmative Action and Diversity Policies", Alexandra Kalev, Frank Dobbin, and Erin Kelly go over the success of various types of affirmative action and efforts towards minority equality, as well as racial quotas and diversity initiatives. These initiatives focus on both hiring a more diverse workforce and ensuring that diversity hires have an equal path to managerial positions. Aside from working apart biases, many of these efforts includes aspects that would encourage open social capital flow for everyone. While the idea of most of these programs are good, often diversity initiatives fail to address the problem and instead force individual solutions. The study: "The argument that organizations should structure responsibility for reducing inequality may seem commonsensical, but today's popular diversity programs often focus on changing individuals…Theorists prescribe solutions that change incentives for, and beliefs of, individuals with the idea that most problems of management are problems of motivation rather than structure." Not enough diversity efforts are aimed at tackling a "biased foundation" and instead tweak individual instances. In short, these solutions need more of a focus on structural capital. The patterns a company develops need to change.

Kalev, Dobin, and Kelly noted a consistent effective tool was having a governing body, such as Lyndon Johnson's creation: The Office of Federal Contract Compliance Programs, instruct businesses to form and then enforce their own yearly diversity goals. Organizations were often "wildly optimistic" about what they could achieve. And the successes or failures of both affirmative action and the Office of Federal Contract Compliance are questionable at best.

Overall, programs such as minority quotas, have not solved problems, and occasionally resulted in significant strife by harming bonding social capital within companies. The numerous proposed solutions to homogeneity, especially in business leadership; are mostly variations on those two ideas. If there is one right answer to end complications stemming from ingroups in business and elsewhere, no business leader seems to have found it yet.

Legal Fixes

There are other sectors of society who have made significant contributions towards enforcing equality in America. While very far from perfect, U.S. courts are powerful agents of change, and a fair justice system would pave the way for national righteousness. Numerous cases over several centuries have signified American racial progress—or a lack thereof.

Going through the entire legacy of a court ricocheting from pro-discrimination to pro-reform would be excessive. However, a few major historical decisions include the 1857 *Dred Scott v. Sandford* ruling which enshrined someone enslaved as their master's legal property. 1948's *Shelly v. Kramer* was a victory in which the Supreme Court ruled that lower courts may not enforce laws restricting property rights based on race. Of course, the most famous race case in history is 1954's *Brown v. Board of Education of Topeka*, in which the court made all "separate but equal" laws illegal, effective ending the Jim Crow era in America.

The same history applies to gender-based decisions. These include 1923's *Adkins v. Children's Hospital* in which the Supreme Court struct down a federal law maintaining a minimum wage for women. 1965's *Griswold v. Connecticut* defended women's rights to obtain contraceptives in any circumstance, including marriage. Of course, for all concerned, 1973's *Roe v. Wade* is the most controversial, as it ensures a woman's right to have an abortion.

More recently, the Supreme Court has made strides towards implementing fixes which might contribute to equality in the workplace and society in general. 2016 saw a defense of affirmative action when a lower court decision *Fisher v. University of Texas* was overturned on the basis that a racial preference for college admittance was not unconstitutional. Justice Anthony Kennedy, the author of the majority opinion wrote, "A university is in large part defined by those intangible qualities which are incapable of objective measurement, but which make for greatness…Considerable deference is owed to a university in defining those intangible characteristics, like student body diversity, that are central to its identity and educational mission." This ruling secured the right for a public institution, such as a state university, to practice affirmative action, and sanctioned it as constitutional behavior. *Fisher v. University of Texas* protected and extended diversity-based practices, not just based on race, but gender and other minority statuses as well.

In 1964, the Supreme Court ruled on *Price Waterhouse v. Hopkins*, and recorded that employee discrimination based on sex stereotypes was unlawful. Ann Hopkins was a senior partner at a law firm repeatedly overlooked for a partner position due to her gender. While her case did not pass muster at lower courts, the Supreme Court found that her lack of promotion violated Title XII of the 1964 Civil Rights Act. Hopkins faced numerous impediments to success, but ultimately buttressed female workers' jobs everywhere.

While not specifically about social capital, these decisions took steps towards enforcing equality in company practices. Making sure individuals get the same opportunities to advance guarantees free flow of personnel and encouraging diversity in higher-education institutions evens academic chances. If a person is not on even footing with their coworkers, they will be treated as if they are less deserving of trust and other social capital-building instincts. These laws do not just defend employees' money and career ascension, they defend their ability to harness networks of reciprocity to become more efficient and better-equipped to fulfill their duties. The American legal system is not perfect by any stretch, evidenced in part by the numerous missteps by lower courts in these cases, but decisions to back people here, fights structural inequality on a fundamental level.

Religious Fixes

Apart from business policy and legal instruction, social capital equality is equalizing through religion. Devout people in the service of the same spirituality find common ground which can overcome huge social barriers. Being pursuant of such an ethereal construct requires a specific disposition. People who are believers overlook many differences, such as ethnicity or class, to find equality with others who share their faith. Whether it is Christians and Christians, Muslims and Muslims, Buddhists and Buddhists, or most similar world religions, where there is piety, there is connectivity. (Sects within religions, most notably Sunni and Shiite Muslims, are effectively unique faiths in the context of the other, so this positive connection is not in play.)

Corwin Shmidt wrote *Religion as Social Capital: Producing the Common Good,* concluded the positive effects of religion include generating the illusive bridging social capital between groups of different class but similar faith. "Accepting the current institutional arrangements of the American polity, various studies show how religious communities can offset class and racial bias… and various studies conclude that religion is the predominant institution working against the class bias of American civic engagement because those who are already privileged economically also control a greater portion of the other resources needed for democratic participation." Those "economically privileged" are more disposed to treat others subscribing to the same religious beliefs fairly, even if they might be inclined towards discrimination against the poor.

Sadly, while Shmidt does not cover this in as much detail, the reverse effect is true as well. People who do not share religions are shut out of certain social circles and do not get the social capital opportunities. Churches and synagogues and other religious institutions are often places of community where congregations gather to share one another's company. Missing those opportunities puts non-believers at a disadvantage, possibly a major one if two parties' religions are at odds. Shmidt concludes that religion, at least in America, at least right now, is a net positive for equalizing social capital. Despite the harm faith can cause, overall the good outweighs the bad. Hopefully, he is correct, and religion is a natural social force which will push America in the direction of a healthy, fair society.

Part Three: Foundations of Social Capital

Chapter 12: Philosophies

While the arguments about how to define and address social capital continue to rage on in modern times, the previous section offered the most commonly agreed-upon summation. However, to truly understand those ideas, it is necessary to begin long ago with the first vestiges of social capital theory and move forward in time while exploring the notions of different scholars with numerous backgrounds and influences. These characters assigned different gradients of significance to different aspects of social capital theory; but, they each played a major role in creating a spectrum of modern ideologies, of which this book is now a part.

The true origins of the term are difficult to pin down. As with pretty much every aspect of language, it is always possible to look further back for increasingly deeper influences. However, the derivation of the ideas we are focusing on seems to stem from the German idealist philosopher, Immanuel Kant. Although Kant never used the literal phrase *social capital*, he espoused the value and practicality of social bonds in his 1785 work *Groundwork for the Metaphysics of Morals*. Kantian ethics—the eccentricities of which are a philosophical wormhole beyond the scope of this book—center around an ironclad sense of duty to be moral, including steadfast in your relationships with others. This fed into Kant's ideas regarding the value of connection and would inform generations of future scholars who featured more prominently in the development of the concept of social capital.

Kant was a fascinating character in his own right, who, despite significant physical infirmity, produced some of the greatest and most influential philosophical work the ever to grace the field. He was notorious for his rigorously-enforced living habits, waking up at exactly 5 and going to sleep at 10 nearly every day of his working life. This clocklike routine helped him overcome extensive health problems and engendered his existence with a sense of calm many historians have credited with a significant benefit to Kant's working capabilities.

The absolutism of Kantian ethics appealed to and greatly influenced a 19th century political philosopher who did write at length about all forms of capital: Karl Marx. When searching for the root of many socioeconomic and political concepts, you can usually find Karl Marx's musings (or radical rants, depending on your point of view) on the subject somewhere. Social capital is no exception. While social capital was not the centerpiece of the economic and political ideologies that made him infamous, his work shaped the foundation of what modern thinkers believe about social capital.

Marx probably considered his political ideologies the inevitable extension of Kant's work, but the two could not have been more different in their lifestyle. Where Kant was disciplined in the extreme, Marx worked all hours of the day and night, often while smoking large pipes stupendously stuffed with tobacco. His diet consisted of daily lavish meals, occasionally interspersed with bouts of extensive drinking, some of which he paid for by selling his clothing. Marx's friend, another legendary philosopher, Frederick Engels, ended up funding large portions of his regime. For all that, Marx maintained a massive workload for most of his adult life and gave the world his outlook on political theory.

Marx's use of the phrase social capital was somewhat different from what we have so far gone over. He purported that personal bonds from shared experience could create a framework of solidarity among people, especially the labor class. However, Marx rarely contemplated social capital as a purely economic idea. For Marx, all forms of capital, social capital included, were manipulated by capitalist controllers who used them expressly to maximize profit, regardless of any moral implications. They would employ their capital to exploit the labor of those who had no choice but to follow.

In volume two of *Capital: Critique of Political Economy*, Marx puts forth his own definition of social capital, one of the first in evidence. "Every individual capital forms, however, but an individualized fraction, a fraction endowed with individual life, as it were, of the aggregate social capital, just as every individual capitalist is but an individual element of the capitalist class." To Marx, social capital was a cumulative resource which encompassed virtually every form of economic asset. The sum of human bonds within society was strong enough to master every potential advantage. He included not only what we have called relational capital, structural capital, and cognitive capital, but more concrete forms of capital such as property or wealth. Marx identified the value of what we have discussed but did not separate it as its own category of wealth.

First Examination

If we are looking for the first thinker who identified the value of social capital and used the term roughly the same as we are using it now, Lyda Hanifan is the proper focus. While not nearly as prolific or influential as the likes of Marx or Kant, Hanifan does offer the first real instance of the phrase *social capital* similar to the manner in which it is employed today. He deserves credit as the person who coined the term and as the foundation upon which future thinkers would raise a tower of scholarship.

Born in a late 19th century timbering camp in West Virginia, Hanifan was an unlikely character to take such an important step in sociopolitical theory. Despite a rustic upbringing, he was well-educated at the Universities of Chicago and Harvard. After returning to West Virginia, Hanifan spent most of his adult life working as a state supervisor of rural schools in his home state. His writing came primarily in the form of two little-noticed books and numerous pamphlets directed at local schools, counselling the nearby communities to get involved in education.

Hanifan believed strongly in the value of social networks and, especially, the reciprocal nature of bonds between people living and working close together. He saw these bonds as potential forces for community development. Perhaps due to his humble background and eventual lofty education; during his tenure, Hanifan worked hard to encourage towns to bond for the sake of their children's education.

In his 1916 article, *The Rural School Community Center*, 8 pages in total, Hanifan writes, "In the use of the phrase *social capital* I make no reference to the usual acceptation of the term capital, except in a figurative sense. I do not refer to real estate, or to personal property or to cold cash, but rather to that in life which tends to make these tangible substances count for most in the daily lives of a people, namely, good will, fellowship, mutual sympathy and social intercourse among a group of individuals and families who make up a social unit…"

That was the first identifiable instance of the phrase social capital combined with a semi-modern understanding of its usage. A few years after publication, the phrase, and Hanifan himself, was mostly lost to history. That is, until contemporary scholars dug it up, and gradually social capital became the phrase no economic theorist could stop discussing. No word on how Hanifan's writing influenced West Virginia schools, but it undoubtedly had an impact on academics today.

Chapter 13: Rediscovery and Rethinking

Tracing the course of the study of social capital throughout history is not a simple task. There is never a shortage of thinkers composing their beliefs, and social capital is comprised of many well-trod topics. However, two world wars did stem the tide of discourse somewhat. The best-established instance of the term following Hanifan's coinage occurred almost fifty years later, in 1961, with renowned political activist Jane Jacobs's discussion of it in her book *The Death and Life of Great American Cities*. Jacobs was often more interested with practical causes; namely, the protection of lower-income city dwellers, than high-minded sociological abstractions. However, when Jacobs did take time to set down her principles, her rhetoric was memorable. She wrote, "Cities have the capability of providing something for everybody, only because, and only when, they are created by everybody." These words, not surprisingly, gained her great acclaim, and helped her safeguard the future of many impoverished urban areas.

While Jacobs stopped short of modernity in her exploration of social capital theory, she took it a step further than Hanifan. Jacobs extended the ideas regarding importance of social connections and management of cognitive capital beyond a school environment and focused on city planning. She saw the growth of connectivity in neighborhoods and community participation in government as the inevitable extensions of high social capital.

She does not use the term social capital often, but large portions of the text are taken up with the same language and underlying theory employed by scholars today. One passage reads, "If self-government in the (neighborhood) is to work…there must be a continuity of people who have forged neighborhood networks. These networks are a city's irreplaceable social capital. Whenever the capital is lost, from whatever cause, the income from it disappears…never to return until and unless new social capital is slowly and chancily accumulated…(cohesive neighborhoods) contain many individuals who stay put." What she is discussing here is developing social capital through longevity of connection. Trust builds over time, and with it comes the varying benefits of a responsive network of mutually supportive groups. In Jacobs's vision, social capital is the cornerstone of well-developed city life.

Jacobs also explored ideas we would classify as structural capital, although not to as great an extent. She believed in the value of infrastructure and making community resources available to all citizens. The government was, of course, a collaborative actor in this sense; working alongside the populous to create a functioning city. This is not unlike the function of pre-established structural capital interacting with fresh cognitive capital within a business. Tentpoles of the surrounding environment, in this case the foundational institutions upon which a community is built, shape the growth of ideas.

Jacobs had not made the move towards a business-facing version of social capital or the more personal takes on an individual's social capital which grew from later European thinkers. However, her work invited scrutiny, which quickly lead numerous other thinkers from different fields to consider the applications of social capital in the marketplace. How might having social capital help a workplace function, or retain customers, or build new ideas?

The Next Wave of Scholarship

Jacobs's usage of social capital in her writing on city development quickly caught the eye of other scholars who transferred the idea into broader use. In 1969, a few years after her article gained recognition in higher sociological circles, a man named Robert Salisbury wrote an article "Exchange Theory for Interest Groups" for the *Midwest Journal of Political Science,* expanding on Jacobs's ideas. A young political science professor at Washington University, Salisbury recognized the importance of reciprocity within groups trying to succeed in a highly-competitive environment.

However, whereas Jacobs looked at neighborhood life within cities, Salisbury saw a model for party unity in politics. He wrote, "...incentives consist of the realization of suprapersonal goals, goals of the organization or group. Although, of course, the benefits of such achievement may accrue to particular individuals, they are not ordinarily divisible…thus 'peace' or 'states' rights' or 'civil liberties' are all desired by individuals…and they benefit from entering into positive relationships with individuals with shared values…" Salisbury goes on to describe the issues plaguing political organizations; namely, that people are working simply in tandem, not as a unified group of people with shared objectives. He saw the main problem in politics as a lack of strong interpersonal relationships; what we would call relational capital.

Soon on Salisbury's heels was Pierre Bourdieu, a titanic figure in sociological theory, and hugely-influential political thinker in France for many years. His scholarly contributions to the two fields of study were largely data-driven. Bourdieu believed in quantifying as much as possible. He brought mathematical vigor to his work and was one of the first to attempt to calculate the value of social capital (although some scholars have argued that he found limited success in this effort).

The idea of social capital came to Bourdieu by way of Karl Marx, whose work he discovered to be a great influence. Marx's insistence on the importance of societal networks as a way of conveying value shows up numerous times in Bourdieu's writing. However, while Marx stayed firmly entrenched in pure theory of economics, Bourdieu found applications in other parts of cultural operations, including the importance of social capital to business. (It is, of course, crucial to bear in mind certain scholars who came before; specifically, Jane Jacobs, who Bourdieu almost certainly read or at least knew of. However, he does not mention her in his literature, and Marx comes up often.)

Bourdieu's main contribution to the library on social capital was his appraisal of its ability to hold value longer than other types of capital, which he espoused first in 1972 in *Outline of a Theory of Practice*. He saw money and property as secondary and even transient in comparison, emphasizing the ability of the rich to stay rich despite setbacks, such as numerous business failures, which would permanently impoverish many others. He believed, simply, that once a person or group of people reached a threshold level of social capital with their peers and within their organizations, their economic position was largely secure. In *A Social Critique of the Judgement of Taste,* Bourdieu wrote, "To a given volume of inherited capital there corresponds a band of more or less equally probable trajectories leading to more or less equivalent positions…the skill in operating connections enables the holders of high social capital to preserve or increase this capital…"

Bourdieu was the son of a sharecropper in the south of France, and his modest beginnings left him with a lifelong distaste for the upper crust of society. Often, he was known to repeat the words, "Every established order tends to make its own entirely arbitrary system seem entirely natural." However, despite his aversion, Bourdieu saw that there was value in studying the systems which kept the rich at the top of the societal ladder. Chief among these systems was the tight network of relationships and shared institutions that were exclusive to the rich. More than their money, their social capital protected their status, and facilitated their continued rise.

Unlike many other scholars, Bourdieu did not see social capital as a potential instrument of good. To him, it was symbolic of the gap in experience between rich and poor, and institutionalized inequality in France and across the world. Later thinkers had to expand on Bourdieu's ideas before social capital found its place as a recognized tool of the business world.

Chapter 14: Later Models

Bourdieu's attention, despite the negative spin, was enough to secure social capital a position in scholarly circles around the world. A flood of new work about social capital came out in the following years. Scholars everywhere began to address varying implications of the concept in different areas of society.

In 1976, Glenn Loury, a notable economics professor at Brown, extended Bourdieu's lead on the class implications of unequal social capital to include the economics of racial subjugation in America. Loury saw that minorities were not just unequal economically and the victims of a structured social system, but they were at a disadvantage when it came to forging relationships necessary to success. Not only was their relational capital very low with members of upper-class society who controlled the major institutions necessary for success, most ignored the ability of minorities to contribute to cognitive and structural capital. Artificial limits on many minority workers' ability to generate social capital contributed to a need for policy changes regarding race equality.

Loury's main contribution to the debate came from his Northwestern University discussion paper, "A Dynamic Theory of Racial Income Differences" in which he wrote, "An individual's social origin has an obvious and important effect on the amount of resources which are ultimately invested in his development. It may thus be useful to employ a concept of 'social capital' to represent the consequences of social position in facilitating individual acquisition of the standard human capital characteristics. While measurement problems abound, this idea does have the advantage of forcing the analyst to consider the extent to which individual earnings are accounted for by social forces outside the individual's control." These words generated political controversy, but also caught the eye of a transformative thinker: James Coleman, who directly cited Loury as the cause of his studies.

Coleman, maybe the true father of the modern conception of social capital, spent most of his early life focused on hard science. From graduate study of organic chemistry at Columbia University, he pivoted to sociology and eventually economics after taking a secondary course to fulfil graduation requirements. This turned out to be a fateful choice, as he soon began composing dazzling papers which brought his talent for mathematical precision to sociology. He worked as a professor at numerous prestigious colleges, all the while contributing to education, political science, math, and psychology.

His encounter with Glenn Loury's work did not come until the late 80s. Loury's idea inspired him, and, in 1988, Coleman released "Social Capital in the Creation of Human Capital" in *The American Journal of Sociology*. Here, Coleman offered his definition of social capital, "Social capital is not a single entity, but a variety of different entities having two characteristics in common: they all consist of some aspect of social structures, and they facilitate certain actions of actors whether persons or corporate actors within the structure…unlike other forms of capital, social capital inheres in the structure of relations between actors and among actors. It is not lodged either in the actors themselves or in physical implements of production."

In 1990, Coleman expanded his thoughts to a lengthy book, *Foundations of Social Theory*. Here, he clarifies the main differences between his ideas (somewhat anticipated by Salisbury) and those of Loury and Bourdieu: Coleman took what most saw as a force which could only mark individuals, and incorporated businesses, organizations, and other large-scale actors in society. This affected future thinkers to a significant degree. Many other authors wrote about social capital mainly from the singular perspective, but Coleman saw its potential both for a person and a group of people.

Also, unlike Loury and Bourdieu, Coleman imagined social capital as a resource which could be used beneficially, not as a tool of exploitation. It is productive; that is, unlike money and other forms of capital, social capital over time will multiply itself. More importantly, it makes actions possible that would not be possible otherwise. Social capital is not just attained and then spent, there is fundamental value in its accumulation and holding.

Coleman recognized the value of relationship networks in the working class. While these connections did not so directly shift the levers of power as with the rich, low-income earners gained great value from their own social systems. This harkens back to Jane Jacobs's and even Lyda Hanifan's work. Synthesizing numerous former scholars to create a pure conception of social capital was very much a part of Coleman's legacy.

Putnam

Of all the thinkers that have addressed social capital, Robert Putnam is probably the most responsible for its popularity in economic, sociological, and political spheres of study. Jacobs, Bourdieu, and Coleman are the biggest names that commonly appear in conjunction with the development of the term, but Putnam's work brought it into the public eye.

A career academic, Putnam drew his inspiration from Coleman, citing *Foundations of Social Science* as a central source on which he built his theory. In 1993, Putnam, along with several other researchers, conducted a lengthy study of civic engagement, which Putnam believed was an indicator of a government's social capital, in regional Italian governments. The write-up of the study contains a definition of social capital offered by Putnam and his colleagues: "Social capital here refers to features of social organization, such as trust, norms, and networks, that can improve the efficiency of society by facilitating coordinated actions". Putnam reinforces the importance of reciprocity as the main benefit of social capital, an idea which had only been touched on by scholars before him.

Putnam followed up his 1993 study with Making Democracy Work, a more detailed account of his study. He did not, however, really make his mark until 1995, with the release of "Bowling Alone: America's Declining Social Capital" in the Journal of Democracy, and the subsequent book in 2000, Bowling Alone: The Collapse and Revival of American Community. These publications made him famous enough to feature in People magazine and garner an invitation to meet then President Clinton.

Putnam made two major strides in the study of social capital. First, he divided actions that build social capital into two types: bridging and bonding. Bridging actions occur between people belonging to two different groups, people who are, where the behavior is concerned, from fundamentally different backgrounds. These differences could be based on race, class, regional heritage, or any number of varying differences. A bridging action could happen between players on different sports teams. Bonding behaviors are just the opposite: connections formed within a group. Bonding social capital many times comes from mutual experiences, such as shared heritage or patterns of life experience.

Both facilitated social capital, but they affected society in very different ways; both could be helpful or hurtful, according to Putnam. He writes, "Bonding social capital constitutes a kind of sociological superglue, whereas bridging social capital provides a sociological WD-40. Bonding social capital, by creating strong in-group loyalty, may also create strong out-group antagonism…and for that reason, we might expect negative external effects to be more common with this form of social capital.

Nevertheless, under many circumstances, both bridging and bonding social capital can have powerfully positive social effects." Putnam has taken the middle-ground when it comes to his view on the "goodness" of social capital. He does not see it as purely a force for the upper class and the talented to maintain control over the less fortunate, like Loury and Bourdieu. Considering that every active member of society is part of numerous social networks, that is a somewhat one-dimensional view. But, Putnam also clearly saw the exclusion, mistrust, and even bigotry of overly-bonded social groups displayed.

Second, for most his academic career, Putnam had made it known that he believes American society is failing, largely due to a lack of social capital. Civic engagement is regularly very low compared to other developed countries, something which Putnam believed was an indicator Americans no longer trust in their government and have discarded basic relationships with the institutions that have protected and guided them in the past. Further, technology has eroded American life, and significantly closed us off from other people. Putnam saw what he dubbed "thin trust" and "thick trust", or two different degrees of relational capital that a bond can exist in. "Perhaps thick trust—confidence in personal friends—is as strong as ever…However, thin trust—the tenuous bond between you and your nodding acquaintance from the coffee shop, that crucial emollient for large, complex societies like ours—is becoming rarer." For Putnam, the decay of social capital-based networks was responsible for many of the problems in society.

Putnam has continued to promote his view of American social capital to this day, even starting projects devoted to restoring institutions and behaviors to points of higher social capital. (A quick criticism before we move on: while his analysis is cogent, especially where his predictions of dire implications of over-bonded political groups are concerned, there are places where it falls short. This is notably true when it comes to underestimating the power of online communities to create modern forms of "thin trust" that he believes to be so crucial. These networks have led to great positive impact that wouldn't have been possible in the pre-internet age.) Putnam is a political scientist, and so focuses largely on societal behaviors. We're here to cover social capital's applications in the business world, so it is necessary to continue a little further down the road of analysis to look at Putnam's contemporaries in the new millennium.

Chapter 15: Modern Economic Thought

Many modern scholars credited with taking social capital as far as it has gone in the business world probably were introduced to the concept through Robert Putnam's work, but most were—and are—notionally closer to James Coleman. Coleman conceived of social capital as a harvestable resource, something which an alert person could cultivate to their advantage. He also wrote that social capital could be collective; groups could gain or lose social capital like a person, either based on mass actions on the actions of a representative.

Numerous thinkers took those ideas and applied them to running a business and being an entrepreneur. Of course, many ran them through the perspective of influential economic theorists, notably one of the true founders of economics: Adam Smith. Smith never used the term social capital; but, in his first discourse on free markets, *The Theory of Moral Sentiments,* he considered the impact of relationship networks on free markets. Smith saw the tremendous potential influence of what we now call social capital if a business knew how to use it correctly.

In 2005, Christian Waldstrom made headway on the interactions between different types of social capital within one organization. He noted that well-bonded groups with high relational capital can have a great impact on a business's structural capital. However, an individual with strong inter-organizational bridging relational capital can affect significant change as well. For instance, a group of talented individuals who work well together on important projects are hugely influential. However, a well-liked person with a lot of experience in different areas can be a dominant force as well.

There are, of course, numerous groups within a firm that can affect the firm's overall social capital in different ways. The ability to make connections with other employees is hugely important. But, a person's high rank within a firm can give them greater power over structural capital, and a person's intellectual value to the firm gives them greater leverage over cognitive capital.

Social Capital on a Global Scale

Recently, many globalist thinkers have considered the impact of this topic on multinational corporations, who often suffer from a lack of social capital. A large portion of the population view such large entities as "faceless" and "stomping out small business", a reputation that certain corporations have not done very much to dispel. This aversion has squashed many opportunities for multinationals to gather social capital.

In 2004, the Worldwatch Institute described this in their *State of the World* saying, "…low levels of societal trust may lock countries in a 'poverty trap,' in which the vicious circle of mistrust, low investment, and poverty is difficult to break…(the World Values Survey) found that each 12-point rise in the survey's measure of trust was associated with a 1 percent increase in annual income growth, and that each 7-point rise in trust corresponded to a 1 percent increase in investment's share of (gross domestic product)." Large corporations—as well as some government institutions—looking to invest in new markets found their plans went much more smoothly when they formed social capital with people early in their initial investment period. Tatianna Kostova, writes in her 2002 paper "Social Capital in Multinational Corporations: A Micro-Macro Model of its Formation" that "It is well-recognized in the literature that among the most critical tasks in multinational corporations are the extensive coordination, integration, and exchange of recourses between and among various countries."

The Worldwatch report goes on to specify that, aside from trust, which led to significant growth in companies' ability to recruit employees with high cognitive capital, robust social capital created reciprocity with local partners. This (Putnam's "bridging behavior") led to much higher profits and even stronger relationships between multinational corporations and local governments.

Social Capital as a Business Tool

Earlier, we explored the power of social capital to improve market standing through direct relationships with other businesses and customers. Many scholars behind that thinking based their ideas on practical business experience. For that reason, this work is generally focused on applied knowledge, case studies, and rules-based models, as opposed to scholars such as Bourdieu or Salisbury, who wrote pure theory.

Author Jonathon Porritt, in his 2012 book, *Capitalism as if the World Matters*, offers a definition close to what we have proposed: "Capital is a stock of anything that has the capacity to generate a flow of benefits which are valued by humans. Social capital takes the form of structures, institutions, networks and relationships which enable individuals to maintain and develop their human capital in partnership with others, and to be more productive when working together than in isolation. It includes families, communities, businesses, trade unions, voluntary organizations, legal/political systems and educational and health bodies." He goes on to emphasize the importance of social capital as an instrument for the growth and use of other assets.

Increasingly, the academic community started viewing social capital not just as a real asset which could create new opportunities for businesses, but as something which could facilitate the usage of already-held resources. This is largely where relational capital and structural capital interact with cognitive capital. Strong structural capital promotes an efficient and effective work environment where employees have the tools to utilize their cognitive capital. Positive relational capital generates bonds that help employee efforts reach the market in the best possible condition.

In 2001, *In Good Company*, written by scholars Dan Cohen and Laurance Prusak, proposed that social capital grows best organically. Insincere jabs at networking and forced praise of an employee's cognitive contribution do no good. "Networks of social connection, trust, and commitment cannot be manufactured or engineered…social capital thrives on authenticity and withers in the presence of phoniness or manipulation… leaders should not take a hands-off approach to social capital…their interventions must be based on a careful understanding of the social realities of their organizations." To increase social capital within a company, managers must appreciate when to direct their employees and when to allow the workplace to flourish on its own.

The year 2007 saw Alistair Anderson and John Park take social capital a step further into the business world with the publishing of "Entrepreneurial Social Capital: Conceptualizing the Social Capital in New High-Tech Firms". They assert what many scholars had ignored previously: social capital functions differently within general society than it does with an entrepreneur or business. Entrepreneurs are a product of their environment and employees in a company operate according to the same set of societal standards. However, much of entrepreneurial social capital, namely relational capital, is not built on normal relations between identical parties, but relations between consumer and producer, or between different businesses. A simple example: the relationship between you and a person ahead of you in line at a Starbucks is fundamentally different from the relationship between you and the person trying to sell you a used Toyota. When money is changing hands, there is always some disparity in power between people.

In short, the difference between regular social capital and entrepreneurial (or business) social capital, is that the first doesn't have a specific goal, and the second is about making money. Anderson and Park specify their thoughts on how entrepreneurial social capital facilitates those goals. "In entrepreneurship research there is a general consensus that a high level of social capital often assists entrepreneurs to gain access to venture capitalists, key competitive information and potential customers… social capital may also assist by providing and diffusing critical information and essential resources." Social capital can jumpstart a business as sure as financial capital, and, as previously stated, can keep an organization afloat even when the money dries up.

Modern Synthesis

That essentially brings the thinking on social capital current. In the last two decades, since Putnam released

Bowling Alone, many writers have thrown in their two cents on the subject, only adding slight adjustments or addendums. However, most of that was somewhat redundant, or specific to the point of being incomprehensible.

You may have noticed that, while social capital was thoroughly covered in this section, the distinctions between cognitive, relational, and structural subdivisions were not. There are two reasons for this. First, the numerous contradictory accounts of the origin stories for each term combine to form an incomprehensible narrative quagmire in which no scholar would really get credit for anything. Conversely, the timeline of the development of social capital is mostly clear: Marx, Hanifan, Jacobs, Bourdieu, Coleman, and Putnam are the widely agreed upon important figures, and other worthy scholars weave their way through with smaller contributions.

Second, there's not very much point. Of course, it's important to understand the social capital thoroughly, slicing the idea into three smaller sections is only a tool to facilitate that understanding. Knowing those smaller ideas should not be a goal unto itself. Focusing on the relational, cognitive, and structural, instead of the social, is missing the proverbial forest for the trees.

If this sounds somewhat dismissive, it is, at least, not a wholly unique idea. In "Social Capital, Intellectual Capital, and the Organizational Advantage", Oxford professor Janine Nahapiet writes, "We suggest that it is useful to consider (social capital) in terms of three clusters: the structural, the relational, and the cognitive dimensions of social capital. Although we separate these three dimensions analytically, we recognize that many of the features we describe are, in fact, highly interrelated. Moreover, in our analysis we set out to indicate important facets of social capital rather than review such facets exhaustively." Cognitive, relational, and structural capital will continue to be important parts of this exploration, but an excessive analysis of those terms' history will not.

Thanks to the many scholars who provided insight and in-depth contemplation on social capital, we are privileged to have extensive understanding of a force that affects every aspect of our society. From here, we move to the present and future, and what the fate of social capital means for everyone.

Part Four: Practical Contemporary Shifts

Chapter 16: Technology Cuts into Social Capital

One of the most striking trends in recent years, especially since the rapid expansion of internet integration, is the depersonalization of business interactions. Face-to-face time has plummeted, and exchanges on the phone are dropping as well. This loss of real sensory connection makes social capital grow far more slowly, and once captured, it is fragile. And oddly, despite the delicate nature of this commodity, social capital is not treated as something which needs protecting.

In *Social Capital and Information Technology*, Volker Wulf covers his view of the connection between new communication technologies and community building. "In general, the relationship between IT (information technology) and social capital seems to be an ambivalent one…As researchers have also documented, existing IT possibilities that were intended to support communication infrastructures, do not support or create a sense of community." Often, tools meant to create stronger long-range bonds between people by augmenting interpersonal interactions end up taking the place of the real-life bond altogether. The net effect is a society where people know a lot of other people only slightly, and only a few people very well. There is, at the same time, more and less connectedness.

There are several factors driving this shift, the most obvious of which involve recent developments in technology. Communication via email has grown exponentially since its inception, and now eclipses any other way of making a connection. The Radicati Group, a data collection agency, estimated that, in 2005, people sent about 200 billion emails per year. By 2018, that number exploded to 269 trillion. While this number includes mass emails and other non-reply and non-solicited communique, the volume of personal emails is staggering. It is now nearly impossible to function in a business setting without continuous online connectivity.

Even with effective spam filters, many professionals in high demand have difficulty keeping up with emails. Another report from Statista estimated the average office worker receives 121 emails a day, excluding spam. The same report stated that office workers spent about 4.1 hours a day on their emails, or 246 minutes. That's an average of 49 seconds per email; not nearly enough time to form a response that might do more than accomplish the bare minimum required to complete the interaction.

Trying to filter this much information is like trying to pump a fire hydrant through a crazy straw. This tidal wave of communication means most emails receive only a fraction of the recipient's time and nearly none of their concentration. Conversations, when they happen at all, are often reduced to a few sentences. An impersonal contact system becomes even less conducive to human connection as people put significantly lower thought into their replies.

This lack of connection feeds into dissolution of social capital. When relationships are not prioritized, bonding begins to wilt. While it is, of course, true that performance is still paramount—that is, if you do your job you'll gain social capital with your coworkers—ignoring the everyday, personable/human side of face-to-face contact weakens your network of social capital considerably. If a person is spending 49 seconds answering an email, it is unlikely they will pause for pleasantries.

Social Network

Online social networking also holds a huge place in the shift of modern communication and formation of social capital. In an odd twist, numerous past sociologists and economists used the phrase "social network" to describe the system of real-life relationships and connections someone has at their disposal. Historically, utilizing a social network involved personal interactions based on strong, and trusting relationships. A robust social network would maximize a person's efficiency, in some cases, and make tasks that would take hours or days completable in minutes.

Modern use of the phrase, of course, is quite different. Most say social network to obliquely refer to Facebook, Instagram, Twitter or any number of numerous other massive long-distance websites; sites that require no physical interaction or significant connectivity beyond a virtual link with another person. A post-Facebook social network is, in many ways, the polar opposite of a James Coleman or Pierre Bourdieu would consider it to be. Shot in the dark, but they would probably be dismayed. The connections are often so slim and fleeting, calling Facebook a social network is almost a stretch. Threads that unite people are as flimsy as a spiderweb's, and just as breakable.

In truth, when discussing social capital, online connectivity is not all bad. It is hard to ignore the numerous connections between literal strangers that sites like Tumblr or Reddit make possible. Communicating with people solely based on mutual interests, without knowing their name, age, location, or any other pertinent details, is a technological marvel. If someone in Scotland likes the same sports team as someone in California, countless web communities exist for them to cherish every win and grieve each loss together. If a graphic artist in Tokyo and a writer in South Africa meet and want to collaborate, a brilliant comic series might result. There is great utility and entertainment value in harnessing the power of millions of people, coming together around things they are interested in. Proactive online communities can put together creative wonders.

However, those same virtually-anonymous connections easily turn into a mob mentality capable of doing great harm. The instances in which members of social networks decode a person's identity and inflict real-world harm on them due to a perceived slight are too numerous to mention. A particularly nasty behavior is known as "doxing"; in which, following the reveal of a formerly-unknown online personality, perpetrators instruct masses of followers to disrupt another's life in whatever way possible. People have ended up in the hospital because of this, and it is very difficult to stop. In cases like these, it is better for people to be kept anonymous and far apart. Where is the social capital there?

Ultimately, the best results of healthy online social networks lead to significant in-person interaction. The general consensus is that an encounter on a dating site is the most successful when participants meet, and that simple notion should be enough to prove the superiority of genuine, and at the risk of sounding dated, old-fashioned social capital: online social networks are at their best when creating genuine face-to-face in-person relationships. So pro-online meeting "experts" can gripe about the length of the reach of Facebook and Twitter, but, as long as real-life interactions are seen as paramount, those complaints should be ignored. Online social networks might be reigning in terms of popularity right-now, and maybe they will remain on top for good. However, websites will never truly match people talking to one another.

Chapter 17: Supporting the Problem

New technologies are cutting down on social capital between businesses and their customers, and the trends responsible are only likely to increase. Customer support has never been a strong point for joining together consumers and producers. People generally use customer support when something has gone wrong with their product. Interactions, even successful ones, are often neutral at best, and can sometimes be a bad experience for both parties.

However, in generations passed, a great deal if not all customer support occurred in-person or over the phone with people who sold the merchandise. There was a personality to the exchange that could build social capital even if the product was poorly-made. Seeing, or at least hearing, a person directly involves themselves with your problem to try and fix whatever's wrong forms a bond that is impossible to replicate over the phone from thousands of miles away. Scripted responses to most questions do not have any kind of human element.

With the evolution of call centers often located in foreign countries, personality is gone. People with almost no connection to the customer or business handle customer support. Many times, they are reading off prompts for significant portions of the call and they take hundreds of calls every day. This doesn't just create a less-effective problem-solving process, it removes any semblance of personal interaction.

A business has never built social capital with a customer by directing their problems to a faceless service outsourcing company overseas. In a situation in which a company could be building bonds with the people buying their goods, most have chosen to export the process, forgoing their opportunity for social capital in exchange for savings on support costs. While the monetary valuation of social capital is difficult, many companies are not making out nearly as well as they believe with this move. Consistently, studies show that bad customer support experiences have a devastating impact on repeat business and can often turn people away permanently.

Call centers are bad enough, but even they are starting to give way to something more impersonal: automated support programs. Following the rise of computer technology capable of handling simple conversations with people, big companies are building online "chatbots" which will conduct basic problem-solving operations in lieu of a customer support agent. Most businesses creating chatbots to talk to their customers online are doing so as a cost-saving measure. A one-time expense of hiring engineers and writers to build the service, with a small contingent of salaried workers who update and manage it, is large at first, but much less than constant cost of a call center.

This technology functions using the principles of "machine learning". As a user, or users, manually completes tasks or interacts with a program in some way, the computer gathers data and uses that data to predict the user's actions. The more data there is, the better that computer gets at predicting behavior, making it smarter and more helpful. One basic instance of machine learning is predictive text.

When you type a text message in your phone, the Messenger software will eventually suggest what the next words might be based on your past behavior. The more you text, the more accurate the predictions become.

Of course, this is where the problem with machine learning comes in. It is based on predictions of common behavior, but irregular patterns throw the computer off completely. Many people have experienced the annoyance of mistakes in predictive text and autocorrect functions when they accidentally send a text that Messenger has wrongly altered. If you message about football a lot, but one day you text your friend about a good meal, the text may end up read "I just ate the best field goal" thanks to an autocorrect mess up. Chatbots function using a much more complex version of machine learning but are similarly susceptible to its potential problems. Uncommon user interactions can send a chatbot cartwheeling into a completely incorrect response tree; a flaw that is rare in human support.

In truth, chatbots will likely be very common within the next five years, and they will mostly do their job effectively. Some of the best computer engineers of the generation are paid great salaries by big tech companies to lower the error rate for this new technology. Moreover, many products, especially those with a high-tech component, experience a common set of low-level failures with straightforward fixes; in other words, perfect problems for chatbots to help users solve. Computers haven't reached a level where they can assist a customer with advanced problems, but using basic formulas, a chatbot can guide someone through troubleshooting Microsoft Word or an email service. It is also worth noting that good chatbots will produce clear responses almost immediately. No petitioner will end up waiting on-hold for 20 minutes. Barring a system failure or massive and sudden mass influx of service requests, a nearly unlimited number of bots can function at once without servers breaking a sweat.

The one thing, however, that chatbots will never be able to reproduce, no matter their sophistication or processing power, is the human element. No chatbot can replicate the simple influence of another person working to help you solve your problem. Customers can't look a computer in the eye or speak to one on a remotely personal level. People are often remarkably good at identifying something which is fake. (Note: This is only true if it is in their interest to do so. When a fake news story posted on social media fits into a helpful narrative, many people are often happy to be mistaken.) Expensive plastic surgery is often painfully obvious, as are many doctored photos. In movies or television shows, tens of millions of dollars spent on a computer-generated image cannot match the reality of a practical set or effect. The same is true for computers copying humans. We recognize ourselves, and it will be quite a while before any robotic voice can trick people for more than a few seconds.

And people don't like a company trying to dupe them. There is nothing more infuriating than logging on to customer support while believing you are communicating with a human only to realize after a few sentences that you are conversing with a machine. Far from building social capital with customer, chatbots and automated messages tear it down. Companies could be gaining connections with the people buying their goods. Instead they are becoming less-involved; less real.

Other Tech

Chatbots are not the worst of this movement. Most major retail chains have added automated lanes and struck a portion of their baggers and checkout personnel; leaving people to swipe their own purchases. A process normally germane to tons of shopping experiences is now handled with an interaction between you and a machine. So often, these interactions are clunky and unnecessary, but revealed like some great gift to consumers. The reality is that thousands of people across a chain of grocery stores just lost jobs.

This brings up another anti-social capital trend growing today: making customers complete a task that a full-time employee would, until recently, have done for them. Often, this is sold as a way of saving money for the customer or embracing a changing world; however, as with many of these technological shifts, most of the cost-cutting stays with the business in the form of hiring fewer full-time workers. But this is another subject, and so another chapter.

Chapter 18: Crowdsourcing

The emergence of smartphone technology, starting with Apple's release of the iPhone in 2007, quickly became a clear force for society-wide change. A much higher degree of processing power on each device allowed phone applications to harness networks of people in influential ways. At first, most companies used this capability for mostly recreational or convenience purposes; games, dating services, and mobile banking being some of the most prominent examples.

However, as smartphone usage became cheaper and more widespread, some creators saw business opportunities which would tectonically shift the marketplace. Companies like Uber, Rover, and Grubhub, launched apps which functioned on the power of everyone having a computer in their pocket. "Peer-to-peer" business models which could handle a massive influx of workers as well as a high rate of employee turnover started to take hold. In Silicon Valley, the "disruptive innovation" could often be a young programmer's golden ticket to funding from a venture capital firm.

This technology is still making major departures from traditional working models. Some people earn a living only using app-controlled jobs, which sometimes means holding down 3 or 4 part-time jobs at once. Workers have a massively diversified task portfolio, sometimes walking dogs, delivering groceries, and cleaning homes all in the same day. People end up on focusing on several very different tasks for a range of customers and employers in a short period of time. They don't build specialization of a useful skill or grow very much loyalty to one position.

This certainly impacts the way they gather social capital with the company that employs them as well as other workers. If a person is only vaguely connected to their profession through an app and a few emails, has no consistent workplace, and has virtually no personal relationships with colleagues, they will not build social capital with their employer. There is not an interconnectedness or expectation of reciprocity, bonding and bridging social capital are out, and structural capital is virtually all that is propping up any semblance of a relationship between employer and employee.

Take an Uber driver, for instance. After passing an application, car inspection, and background check, an Uber driver is registered with Uber's driver phone application and available to search for and accept riders nearby. Concluding that, aside from occasional email correspondence and performance updates, the driver is not in contact with the company. They have no regular human managers to build connections with. Any contact with other drivers has to be proactive, often found via an online forum like Reddit or Tumblr; only occasionally involving an in-person interaction.

While there is certainly appeal to that kind of independence, many drivers call autonomy an important draw towards the work, imagine the kind of social capital that situation builds, or rather the lack thereof. Compare it to working in an office and networking daily with groups of people on shared goals. Whether you like your coworkers is almost irrelevant considering the stark difference between the two experiences. An office builds far more social capital with its workers than a smartphone app, and so can expect much greater loyalty, accountability, and reciprocity.

Most crowdsourced jobs are for positions which traditionally have transient customer-business relationships, situations where social capital is not built anyway. Uber and other ride-sharing apps are taking the place of taxi services, but that is not a detriment to the customer experience because no one gets to know their cab driver on a regular basis. The same is true of Grubhub and its foray into food delivery and Rover into dog walking. There is not much to lose in relationships as far as these businesses go.

For now, it seems as if most customers are happy with their experiences using these app services, but that is nothing compared to the elation these apps' administrators are feeling. Venture capital money and massive valuations are being thrown around like crazy. In 2016, Rover hit an astounding $5 billion valuation. In late 2017, Airbnb was worth $30 billion. In early 2018, Lyft, a rising Uber competitor for the ridesharing market, was valued at a whopping $15 billion. That is almost paltry, however, compared to Uber's recent high-water mark: $72 billion.

These companies with their millions of users and billions of dollars are here for the long haul. Doubtless, some will sink, and some will float, but the phenomenon of crowdsourcing employment is not going away; the weaker social capital bonds it brings with are going to endure as well.

Chapter 19: Bright Spots

A large portion of this book has been a little gloomy. Technology and modern attitudes are devaluing social capital, an undoubtedly important commodity. However, there are notable examples of companies who have successful worked to up their social capital, both internally and externally, and been rewarded for it in the marketplace.

A prominent instance of the power of robust *bonding* social capital is UPS. The United Parcel Service has a reputation for cultivating a company culture that fosters togetherness and understanding among workers and management. Their company guidelines promote face-to-face interactions in the office and avoiding emails whenever possible. Doing business this way builds up an environment of honest communication. Personal interactions also drive up empathy, which leads to fewer arguments and less resentment between coworkers.

The company also makes a point of eschewing stereotypical teambuilding retreats or exercises. Sending a group of people to play strange games or do trust falls they are required to pretend to be enthusiastic about does very little to buff their enthusiasm for proper paperwork protocol. One-off activities which will only appeal to a small portion of the staff can create far more eye-rolls than new friendships, especially if an office is having already having a difficult time. Of course, an option which might sound more welcome but could be potentially much more disastrous is any activity followed by several hours of an open bar. These events are all social capital pitfalls which could divide an office and throw up communication barriers between workers, and UPS does not entertain them.

It is far more important that workers understand the roles their colleagues fill in the office, rather than on a ropes course, so UPS requires office workers to occasionally attend 3am meetings with overnight delivery staff. It isn't fun for the daytime employees, but nothing will foster relational capital like making a 9-5 person spend time with the night shift folks. Doubtless, they will understand the needs and concerns of that part of the operation to a greater extent; not to mention appreciate their own schedule much more.

This strategy of building internal social capital has paid off. As of mid-2018, the United Parcel Service is the largest shipping company in the U.S. with value skyrocketing in recent years. UPS took in 67.48 billion dollars in 2017 and boasted a significant uptick in net income at 6.72%, almost twice as high as a 3.36% growth in revenue. The variance in the two types of growth indicates a high level of company-wide efficiency, largely due to a well-utilized workforce.

External Social Capital

Of course, as we have seen, social capital with customers is just as operative as social capital inside a business, and no company has been as relentlessly proactive in social capital with their customers as Zappos. As an online clothing retailer, they are already at certain disadvantages in terms of building social capital with customers. The lack of in-person interactions is extremely difficult to overcome. However, Zappos took major steps to do so and quickly grew a reputation for being more customer-focused than almost every other retailer on the market.

First, while call centers for customer service are an unavoidable inconvenience, Zappos does not hire from out of the country. American workers fluent in English are answering the phones. Moreover, after extensive training, service reps are not provided with scripts. Zappos officials state this is to encourage a conversational tone in the calls, and to make the interaction as little of a chore as possible. People prefer to talk to a human being; why give that person a script and make sure they sound more like a robot.

Those measures are certainly an admirable first step, but Zappos has made headlines to a much greater degree because of the extent to which the company reps will go for customers in a special situation. In one case, an unprepared groomsman arrived at a wedding without dress shoes, and, after hearing the details on a support call,

Zappos sent him a pair overnight for free. Another time, a Zappos employee hand-delivered shoes from a rival retailer when Zappos ran out of stock at an inopportune moment. On numerous occasions, they send flowers to customers who are having medical difficulties.

This strategy led to a now-legendary 62,400% growth rate over the course of a decade, and extremely high customer satisfaction and retention rates. Amazon eventually bought Zappos for 1.2 billion dollars, but, despite its unconventional nature, the company remains largely true to its original program. This is in-part due to an inception agreement which guarantees a significant degree of autonomy for Zappos, but to a much greater extent because of consistent financial success. If any company doubts the power of having high social capital with customers, Zappos is a robust rebuttal. They are a modern technology company focused on social capital instead of cost-saving measures and phony gimmicks, and they are raking in revenue.

Imitators

The great and growing power of online services clearly has an industry-wide poor record with social capital. However, it would be outlandish to say that apps or sites are leaving as the predominant business model anytime soon. There are too many competitive advantages, and society is already in the grip of web giants like Google and Amazon.

It is also inappropriate to consider that social capital may become totally a relic of past generations. Social capital is a byproduct of human interaction. By dint of our existence, we must build social capital with someone or something. Therefore, if websites are destined to be the future of business, and social capital is inextricably linked to us, it follows logically that the way in which online businesses build social capital must change.

People may become less physically connected, but we will discover other ways to bond relationally with the business world. We will not find these ways on our own; companies will present us with new opportunities and we will show support with our wallets. Eventually, alternative pathways for social capital will form. Web presence is an ever-shifting phenomenon at the forefront of ingenuity. Shoe stores might all be run purely online soon but what Zappos did without any physical locations surpassed many efforts by conventional businesses. That type of customer-focused thinking will be crucial in the coming decades.

Chapter 20: Changing Approaches

The future of every industry will continue to inexorably shift due to technological advances. Companies must find ways of keeping up with those evolutions, and one oft-ignored pathway is tending enduring social capital networks. Gimmicky, one-off, throwaway ploys with clunky programing and wobbly AI, like faceless service robots in hardware stores or automated grocery clerks, cannot come close to matching the relationship building capabilities of personal interactions. Barrages of emails every day only serve to create numerous strained relationships with weakly-connected people. Businesses which return to certain basic practices focused on creating internal social capital between employees, external social capital with other businesses and a loyal customer base, will flourish in the face of other, larger and better-funded behemoths who neglect this crucial area.

One area which has shown major promise here in recent years is the tactics of major political campaigns. Classic strategies of ad blitzes hoisting up a candidate as a guardian angel and an opponent as a relentless devil are losing ground to directors and representatives that focus on mobilizing volunteers canvasing crucial districts and phone banking key homes. Politicians and their legions of supporters knock on doors *en masse* in an attempt to build social capital with voters. Forget impersonal mailers and spam email, votes really come from face-to-face contact; a person giving up their time to argue their case for a candidate or an issue or an interest group.

Agree with his policies or not, Former President Obama is Exhibit A in proving the power of social capital over cold cash. He started as a community organizer and took that hard-nosed strategy to his major campaigns; at the beginning, going up against big money with thousands of volunteers prepared to have doors slammed in their faces for hours on weekends. It is desperate work, made more difficult by long odds. Slowly, however, with each conversation and every reasoned argument, the candidate and the campaign built social capital. All the ads money could buy could not face down bridging capital with formerly estranged voter groups, not to mention bonding capital which kept a team of political operatives hopeful when their party continued to label them a lost cause.

The power and success of the Obama campaign is changing field organizing across America. While big money and tidal waves of TV ads make impacts, networks of devoted volunteers building social capital for the initiative and the power of candidates canvassing as well can combine to overcome large monetary discrepancies.

Examples like that are crucial to showing people, businesses, and government the potential for social capital, and to ensure that society does not so easily let go of relationships and reciprocal networks. As other high-profile politicians run with a more field-focused strategy, that might bring change in the government sector. However, businesses have yet to learn this lesson, and people are not giving the support of their spending habits to the ones who have. This is largely due to the risks involved when turning to a new, seemingly untested mode of behavior. People and businesses are afraid of a poor return on their spending, and the health of the marketplace is taking a hit.

Some facts contained herein are difficult to bear, but the saving grace of everyone's current socioeconomic predicament regarding social capital is that we are still in control of the market's direction. People, workers, business owners, and voters can direct the course of this country towards favoring positive social capital practices again. We can reject untrustworthy companies, regardless of how low prices might be. We can reject ingrown biases and prejudices and form greater bridging capital with people outside our typical social network. Most importantly, we can reject faceless encounters and anonymous interactions, and demand a society more full of humanity. As messy and imperfect as it is.

Final Note

Yogi Berra, the legendary New York Yankees catcher, often known for his anachronisms once said, "It was impossible to get a conversation going, everyone was talking too much." The wild informal communications of much of the modern business world echo those words completely. When everyone is speaking, no one has time to listen; we waste words in the cacophony of other people, pawning off responses on the tiniest portion of conscious thought, or even on shiny new gadgets that can only begin to imitate the illusive power of human interaction.

At the beginning of the text, we defined social capital as *"a set of various relationships, reputations, and assets, existing within an organization or with its partners and customers, that enable business processes to function as efficiently and effectively as possible."* Amidst the numerous renditions of other thinkers' versions of this definition, a common subtext emerged: equality. Creating a social network bridging gaps between far flung groups of people and doing so with the same level of effort and earnestness as with a more similar person is the most potent use of social capital connections. This outlook combines the protection of bonding capital and the reach of bridging capital; corrupt structural capital cannot stand up to relationships built that way.

For downloadable content and more from
the author, please visit
Indcon.us